A SURE FOUNDATION

Harrison House

Shippensburg, PA

A SURE FOUNDATION

BUILDING YOUR LIFE ON
THE UNSHAKABLE TRUTH OF
GOD'S WORD

Andrew Wommack

A Sure Foundation

Building Your Life on the Unshakable Truth of God's Word

ISBN 978-1-68031-240-9

Ebook: 978-1-68031-260-7

LP: 978-1-68031-261-4

HC: 978-1-68031-262-1

Copyright © 2019 by Andrew Wommack Ministries Inc.

Published by Harrison House Publishers, Shippensburg, PA 17257
www.harrisonhouse.com

1 2 3 4 5 6 7 8 / 26 25 24 23 22 21 20 19

CONTENTS

Introduction 7

Chapter 1   Written by God 9

Chapter 2   This Is True. 19

Chapter 3   Plant the Seed! 27

Chapter 4   Can't Beat God's System. 35

Chapter 5   Great Faith 43

Chapter 6   God's Best. 51

Chapter 7   Sowing and Reaping. 59

Chapter 8   How Do I Change? 67

Chapter 9   Under the Influence 75

Chapter 10   Automatically 81

Chapter 11   Steps and Stages 85

Chapter 12   Deep First. 93

Chapter 13   Communing with Him. 101

Chapter 14   Don't You Care About Me? 109

Chapter 15   Potential 117

Chapter 16   Stay on Track! 125

Chapter 17   Stick with the Word 135

Chapter 18   Root, Then Fruit 145

Chapter 19   Choked. 151

Chapter 20   Less Is More! 161

Chapter 21   A Crisis Situation 167

Chapter 22   Back to the Word!. 175

Chapter 23   A Sick Heart. 183

Chapter 24   Feed Your Faith. 191

Chapter 25   Two Doors 197

Chapter 26   Train Your Mind. 205

              The Last Word 213

              Receive Jesus as Your Savior 215

              Receive the Holy Spirit. 217

              About the Author. 219

INTRODUCTION

The way you view God's Word determines how you'll relate to Him. It determines your faith. The Bible says,

> *So then faith cometh by hearing, and hearing by the word of God.*

Romans 10:17

Our society today doesn't really honor or esteem God's Word. They don't place the value on it that they should. And that devaluation of the Word has crept into the church. Many people who call themselves Christians also don't value the Word of God like they should. If somebody asked them if they believed the Bible is God's Word, they would probably answer, "Oh yes, I believe the Bible is God's Word." But when it comes right down to it, they don't understand or esteem the Word very much.

If Satan can attack the Word of God and get you to doubt it to any degree, then the foundation of your faith will crack. It'll fall apart. Everything in the Christian life is built upon the way you view God's Word. To walk by faith and not by sight, you need a sure foundation in the Word of God!

That's why A Sure Foundation is the very first course I teach our new students at Charis Bible College. I take four class periods and instruct them concerning the integrity of God's Word. My aim and goal is to make sure that every person coming to school begins with the right attitude toward the Word of God.

YOU'RE INVITED!

This isn't something that you just accept completely by faith. The Word itself teaches us about its own integrity. God's Word gives us instruction and tells us how important the Word of God should be in our lives.

That's why I want to invite you to join me on this journey of discovery. Your faith will be strengthened and your relationship with God deepened. If you can accept and wholeheartedly receive the truths that I'll be sharing with you from the Word, it'll make a huge difference in your life. You'll experience true growth and be propelled toward greater stability, maturity, and fruitfulness in your Christian life. And as you stand against the wiles of the devil, you'll find yourself standing firm upon a sure foundation!

Chapter 1

WRITTEN BY GOD

Many Christians today think that the Word is just a vague representation of what God really wanted to say. They believe it's been corrupted and mistranslated by people. But that's not what the Bible teaches about itself.

All scripture is given by inspiration of God, and is profitable for doctrine, for reproof, for correction, for instruction in righteousness.

2 Timothy 3:16

The phrase *"given by inspiration of God"* was translated from the Greek word *theopneustos*. This Greek word is a compound word made up of *theos* and *pneo*. According to *Strong's Concordance*, the word *theos* means "a deity, especially . . . the supreme Divinity," and the word *pneo* means "to breathe hard."

Therefore, the word *theopneustos* literally means God breathed. The *Amplified Bible*, the *New International Version*, and *The Message* all render this Greek word as *"God-breathed."* God inspired men to write the Scriptures. They were moved by God as they wrote.

This is a very clear statement that the prophecies of the Old Testament were not just the opinions of people. Instead, they were God-breathed utterances, which can be totally trusted and relied upon.

The Word of God reveals that men wrote as they were inspired and supernaturally moved upon by the Holy Spirit.

> *Knowing this first, that no prophecy of the scripture is of any private interpretation. For the prophecy came not in old time by the will of man: but holy men of God spake as they were moved by the Holy Ghost.*
>
> **2 Peter 1:20-21**

Regarding the Greek word translated *"moved"* in this verse, W.E. Vine said this word signifies "that they were 'borne along,' or impelled, by the Holy Spirit's power, not acting according to their own wills, or simply expressing their own thoughts, but expressing the mind of God in words provided and ministered by Him" (*Vine's Expository Dictionary of Old and New Testament Words*).

There's a whole realm of study called apologetics where people actually use multitudes of facts to logically and intellectually prove the infallibility of God's Word. They go into detail to show how the Bible is truly written to us by God. It wasn't written by men who made errors as they wrote their own thoughts down, and now we have to pick and choose which parts are of God and which parts are of man. No, the Bible is God speaking to us through man. Certain individuals have devoted their entire careers and ministries to this type of endeavor. They show us how hundreds of prophecies spoken in the Word of God have been and, in some cases, are being perfectly fulfilled, even down to the very last detail! This means there is no doubt that the Scriptures are God breathed and God inspired.

Many people today have actually put more faith in such things as science, archaeology, history, mathematics, and medicine than the inspired Word of God. They challenge the record of the Bible, especially concerning certain people groups and locations, contending that they didn't really exist. However, time and time again, as new and more evidence is discovered, the doubters have been proven wrong, and the Word of God has been proven right.

WHICH ONE IS TRUE?

Because we don't have the original manuscripts that the Old and New Testaments were written in—rather, we have copies of copies that our English translations are based upon—intellectuals challenged and assaulted the Word of God, contending,

"It's not accurate. Therefore, we can't trust it. We can't believe it." So, there were people who adhered to the Word and others who believed the intellectuals. But the question remained, "Which is true?"

Think of this: Jesus and the apostles were not using the original documents when they quoted from the Old Testament. They were referencing the Greek Septuagint translation, which was made between two and three centuries after the original documents and between two and three centuries before their time. So, it had been around five or six centuries since the original Scriptures had been written, yet Jesus and the apostles had total confidence that the Greek translation was the Word of God.

Consider these facts:

- Jesus quoted the Greek Septuagint three times when dealing with the devil in the wilderness (Matt. 4 and Luke 4), and it worked, defeating Satan every time.

- Paul likewise quoted the Greek Septuagint. In fact, his letter to the Galatians was centered largely around a single letter in this translation. Paul based his whole argument in Galatians 3 on the word *"seed"* instead of *"seeds"* (Gal. 3:16).

Jesus and Paul believed the inspiration of the Scriptures was preserved even through a translation, down to a single letter of a word.

References to *"the holy scriptures"* (Rom. 1:2 and 2 Tim. 3:15) also highlight this point. God's Word—what we call the Bible—is inspired and preserved by Him so that we can partake of His divine nature (2 Pet. 1:3-4). Without God's Word, we will not partake.

The Dead Sea Scrolls were discovered between 1946 and 1956, providing much evidence concerning the accuracy of the Bible. These scrolls were very ancient compared to the more modern manuscript copies that our translations were based upon. Yet when the experts went back and compared them, most of the differences were insignificant—consisting mainly of minor brushstrokes, which made no substantive differences.

But in checking the few differences that had any substance, like a word being misspelled or a different word substituted, the Dead Sea Scrolls still confirm the accuracy of what we have today. In the book of Isaiah, out of supposedly hundreds of possible differences, things that could have made any real difference were whittled down to about five when studied and explained. So, even though our manuscripts were generations removed from the originals, the Dead Sea Scrolls verified the accuracy of the Word in a way that leaves no doubt that God has been behind it.

The Bible is unique in several ways among all books that have ever been written. First of all, it was written over a period of about 1,400 years by approximately forty different people. Writers came from multiple nations and from totally different walks of life, and they spoke multiple languages. No other book can claim that.

The Bible is also unique and unequaled in the impact it has had on the world. No other book has shaped civilization as much as the Bible, nor has any book been published more or been translated into more languages. Over four billion copies of the Bible have been sold worldwide, with twenty million copies sold each year in the US alone. The Bible has been translated into 2,200 languages and dialects, reaching over 90 percent of the world's population.

Certainly, people's misuse of the Bible has caused many problems, but the good far outweighs the bad. And the bad wasn't the fault of the Bible but rather people's misinterpretation of Scripture for their own personal agendas.

The sheer volume of manuscripts of the Bible compared to any other writing in history is a great testimony to its accuracy.

If you didn't have an original document but had two copies of the original and there were differences between those copies, there would be a fifty/fifty chance that one of the copies was correct. If you had four copies of an original document and three of them were the same, there would be a 75 percent chance that the three were correct.

There are thousands and thousands of manuscripts and scrolls of the Bible, around 24,000 manuscripts of the New Testament alone. This gives us phenomenal confidence in the accuracy of the copies. Many historical documents—documents upon which we base much of our knowledge of history—are accepted without question with only eight to twenty copies in existence. There is infinitely more proof of the life and ministry of Jesus than there is that Julius Caesar existed, yet there isn't disbelief about Julius Caesar. This speaks to the power of Scripture and Satan's fear of and fight against the Bible. There is demonic opposition to Scripture, and those who disbelieve the Bible are under that demonic influence.

The ancient book that is closest to the Bible in the number of manuscripts is Homer's *Iliad*. The *Iliad* has fewer than 1,900 copies of the original document. From a mathematical perspective, the sheer volume of New Testament copies guarantees, with 99.5 percent confidence, that the translation has been preserved.

These relatively fewer copies of Homer's *Iliad* have several hundred lines in question, while the 24,000 copies of the New Testament have only a few dozen lines in question, none of which makes any substantive difference. The closest copy of the *Iliad* was written five hundred years after Homer's original, while the closest copy of the New Testament scriptures was written less than fifty years after the originals.

This means that many who witnessed the events recorded in the New Testament were still alive when the earliest copies were made. If the copies were in error, some eyewitness would surely have discredited them. That didn't happen. Just the opposite is true. These copies were widely used while eyewitnesses were still alive, and the silence of these eyewitnesses is confirmation of the accuracy of these documents.

I've read that because the Bible was quoted so often by ancient writers, all but eleven verses of the New Testament could be reconstructed from these other writers, even if no copies had been made. That's phenomenal! There is no other writing in the history of mankind that has this kind of authenticity. Yet many will accept other documents as authentic with infinitely less authority while rejecting Scripture. That's not intellectually honest. Because of the spirit of antichrist, there is a prejudice or skepticism toward Scripture that doesn't exist toward other documents. That spirit is alive today and working against everything godly.

So, if you want to know more about these natural facts that affirm and confirm that the Bible is indeed true, I encourage you to look into what's called apologetics. Those involved in apologetics go into detail and show important evidence in different fields of study. Although apologetics isn't my strong suit or my point, we do arrive at the same conclusion: The Word of God is not fallible. It's infallible. It's written by God!

LOTS OF ERRORS?

You might be saying, "Oh no, there are thousands of mistakes in the Word of God." Well, I'll admit that the word *music* is spelled *musick* in the *King James Version* of the Bible. And people claim, "That's wrong." No, it's not. It's just an ancient spelling, and that's not an error or a mistake.

When people say there are lots of errors in the Word, I say, "Well, show them to me." I've had people cite Exodus 20:13 before, which says, *"Thou shalt not kill."* Then they'll compare that to Matthew 19:18, which says, *"Thou shalt do no murder."* They argue, "See, right there. That's wrong. In the Old

Testament it says *'kill,'* and in the New Testament, Jesus used the word *'murder.'*"

But the exact same Greek word that was translated *"murder"* in Matthew 19:18 was translated *"kill"* in Mark 10:19 and Luke 18:20, where Jesus said, *"Do not kill."* I believe the Lord inspired the translators to do this because there is no one English word that adequately conveys the original meaning of the Hebrew word translated *"kill"* in Exodus 20:13.

If "kill" was interpreted in the strictest sense, then killing animals for food or sacrifice would be forbidden. We would also be prohibited from defending ourselves or engaging in godly wars, which Scripture abundantly justifies.

Likewise, if "murder" was interpreted in the strictest sense, then things such as negligent homicide would be allowed because they do not include malice aforethought (Ex. 21:28-29 and Deut. 22:8).

The original languages that the Bible was written in, Hebrew and Greek, are more descriptive and expressive than our English language. So, if God had consistently said *"Thou shalt not kill"* in Exodus 20:13 and Matthew 19:18, then that would have ruled out self-defense and killing animals, along with a lot of other things that the Bible verifies and shows as acceptable. Or, if both verses had been translated as *"Thou shalt do no murder,"* then that's not the total intent of what God said either, because murder means to harm a person with malice aforethought. In other words, it's premeditated and planned.

A Perfect Representation

When we put *"Thou shalt not kill"* (Ex. 20:13) together with *"Thou shalt do no murder"* (Matt. 19:18), we can see that the Word of God is a perfect representation. It's a commentary on itself. While translating *murder* or *kill* alone would not have sufficed, by using two different words in two different places and combining them together, we come up with the mind and heart of God. They modify and complete each other, thus painting a fuller picture.

This is the integrity of God's Word, and it's the sure foundation you need in order to know that the Bible is accurate and trustworthy. And if you expect to grow and be fruitful as a believer in Christ, you need to get to where you are adamant about this truth. God's Word is Him speaking to you!

Chapter 2

THIS IS TRUE

The Word of God has to be the foundation of our relationship with God. If we don't trust the Bible, then we cannot really have any assurance in our relationship with the Lord. Personally, I believe God's Word is trustworthy, and we can be absolutely assured. I've verified this in my life millions of times by experience. But for people who don't believe in the Word of God, this is the reason that they don't ever come to a place of declaring, "This is true."

Our society today has moved away from absolute belief in the Word of God. What's the result? What has taken its place? Relativism, which is an idea that what is true for you is not necessarily true for me. There are no absolutes. Therefore, it's politically incorrect in our society for someone to be absolutely sure about anything. To have that attitude today—that there is absolute truth—is looked down upon and considered arrogant.

But the truth is that there are absolutes. God's Word is Him absolutely speaking to us. That's why it can give you a confidence and an assurance that is necessary for spiritual maturity. If you're going to be someone whose interpretation of what is right and wrong changes based on circumstances or what kind of situation you're in, then you're like a ship without an anchor. You're going to float and be driven about and tossed!

> *But let him ask in faith, nothing wavering. For he that wavereth is like a wave of the sea driven with the wind and tossed. For let not that man think that he shall receive any thing of the Lord. A double minded man is unstable in all his ways.*
>
> **James 1:6-8**

When you waver in your faith, you're double-minded. You're hindered in receiving from God. You must have the Word of God as an anchor in your life!

ABSOLUTELY WRONG!

I'm not going to mention names, but a recent former president of the United States of America—who claimed to be a Christian—was notorious for his sexual immorality. If you're familiar with the situation, I'm sure you know who I'm talking about. As some of his liberal beliefs were made public, the news media asked him how he could justify his liberal position but claim to be a Bible-believing Christian.

His answer reflected the attitude of many people today. He said that the Bible is God's Word, but men wrote it based on the circumstances and society they lived in at the time. And all of the values, commandments, and rules about how to conduct oneself are relative to the time. So, because we live in a different time, we have to interpret everything. In other words, he didn't believe in the infallibility of the Word. Like so many today, this man believed it was outdated, it had to be updated, and it had to relate to our times. That is absolutely wrong!

You may disagree, but before you toss this book aside, let me ask you a question: How does your life and experience compare with mine? I know I'm not the perfect standard, but compare the results you're getting to mine. At one time in my life I was an absolute introvert. I couldn't look at a person in the face and talk to them. But now I speak to millions and millions of people over the television, radio, and internet. Also, I used to be terribly fearful and insecure, but that has changed. Now I am a secure person, and I'm not afraid of anything. God changed my life! God has blessed me, and love dominates my life.

A number of years ago, my wife and I were evacuated from our house because of raging wildfires nearby. We live up in the mountains of Colorado, and there was a good chance of me losing my house. But I would tell people, "We got the pictures that can't be replaced, but all the rest of it is just stuff. It doesn't matter." I believed my house would be spared, and during the trial, I refused to be discouraged, beaten down, or worried.

THE DIFFERENCE

As we were driving away from our house, my wife commented, "We've enjoyed these things. And I know we're blessed and believing for the house to be protected. But if we lost everything, it's just stuff. It would be fun to start all over and do it again." I agreed. Where did our stability come from in the midst of this fiery trial? The Word of God. It's our belief in the Word of God that gives us stability in life.

Would you have had that same attitude?

I'm not trying to brag on myself. I pray you understand what I'm saying. I'm bragging on Jesus and what He's done in my life. And I'm saying this because I believe His promises and have lived them out multiple times. My life has been changed. I'm secure. I am one happy person. And I'm blessed. Not only have I seen these emotional and mental changes in my life, but I've seen people raised from the dead and healed. My own son rose from the dead after being gone for five hours. I've seen blind eyes and deaf ears open. I've seen people come out of wheelchairs and marriages put back together. I've seen people harmonized who were at variance with each other. And it's all because of the faith that comes through God's Word!

Now, take what I'm experiencing and put that up against what you're experiencing. Are you a sick, bitter, poor, afraid, insecure person and yet proclaiming, "I don't believe in the Word of God; that stuff is foolishness"? Maybe you ought to look at the fruit that your kind of mindset is producing versus somebody who is living a victorious life. Again, I'm not perfect. I'm still growing. I haven't arrived, but I've left. I'm not claiming that everything in my life is the way it should be, but I'm saying it is infinitely better than it used to be. And I'm telling you, the difference is the Word of God!

God's Word has become more real to me than the word of my father, my mother, my friends, a doctor, a lawyer, politicians, etc. Of course, nearly anybody could say that God's Word is more secure than a politician's, but I'm saying that God's Word has become foundational in my life. Look at the fruit it's producing!

ARGUMENT OR EXPERIENCE?

Some people say, "You just have your head in the sand." Well then, why don't you stick your head in the sand too if it's going to set you free, raise your children from the dead, and bless and prosper you? Get a life! Wise up. Recognize that if what you're doing isn't working, then maybe you ought to change. And if what I'm doing is working, then maybe you ought to stop criticizing and come over to my side.

I'm not trying to be mean. I'm just trying to tell you that our society today has become so intellectual and sophisticated that we think someone is absolutely stupid to just believe in the Word of God, use it as their foundation, and base their life on promises that were written thousands of years ago. Well, I'm telling you that I'm one person who has done that. I haven't done it perfectly, so I may not have perfect results. But to the degree that I have based my life on the Word of God, it's working. It's changing me, and it's setting me free.

You can sit there and argue doctrine. You can show me something you read. You can come at me any way you want to, but you can't change what has happened in my life. You're going to have to come out and call me a liar if you contend that what I'm saying about my son being raised from the dead, multiple people being raised from the dead, blind eyes and deaf ears being opened, people coming out of wheelchairs, and my own radical deliverance from fear, shame, embarrassment, hurt, and pain isn't true. You can sit there and argue with my doctrine all you want, but I'm telling you from personal experience that this is my testimony. My faith and my absolute assurance in God's Word as being true have revolutionized my life. I credit everything good in my life—my salvation, my deliverance, joy, peace, security, miracles—to God's Word.

A person with an argument will never win against a person with an experience. You can sit there with your argument, but I've experienced God's Word. It works. It's real. You're too late to tell me that God's Word is wrong, was mistranslated, and doesn't mean what it says. I've lived it. I've lived those verses, and now I'm encouraging you!

SUCCEED OR FAIL?

Your attitude toward the Word of God determines whether you succeed or fail. It really does.

> *So then faith cometh by hearing, and hearing by the word of God.*
>
> **Romans 10:17**

If Satan can attack your mind and get you to doubt the accuracy and infallibility of God's Word, then he can get you to doubt God.

Chapter 3

PLANT THE SEED!

The foundation of our faith has to be God's Word. Not only must we believe what's there, but we must also believe that God supernaturally communicated His Word to us.

Jesus taught ten parables during His longest day recorded in the New Testament (see my free Online Bible Commentary [awmi.net] or my *Life for Today Study Bible and Commentary: Gospels Edition* for details). In every one of the parables (see Matt. 13, Mark 4, and Luke 8), He was talking about the importance of God's Word in our lives.

This parable in Mark 4 wasn't a random teaching. Jesus was intentionally laying a foundation by constantly talking about the importance of God's Word.

> *Hearken; Behold, there went out a sower to sow:*
> *And it came to pass, as he sowed, some fell by the way*

side, and the fowls of the air came and devoured it up. And some fell on stony ground, where it had not much earth; and immediately it sprang up, because it had no depth of earth: But when the sun was up, it was scorched; and because it had no root, it withered away. And some fell among thorns, and the thorns grew up, and choked it, and it yielded no fruit. And other fell on good ground, and did yield fruit that sprang up and increased; and brought forth, some thirty, and some sixty, and some an hundred.

Mark 4:3-8

HOW THE KINGDOM WORKS

Jesus gave this parable about a man who was going out, taking seed, and just throwing it everywhere. In verses 14 through 20, Jesus interpreted this parable for His disciples and said, *"The sower soweth the word"* (Mark 4:14).

I'll come back and look at this passage in more detail later on. But for now, I want you to see that God's Word is a seed.

Jesus wasn't talking about how to be a farmer. And He wasn't really explaining how seeds grow. The Lord was using a natural illustration that people were well acquainted with to show how the kingdom of God works.

*And he said, So is the kingdom of God, as if a man
should cast seed into the ground.*

Mark 4:26

In the natural realm, you cannot grow anything without a
seed. Everything grows from a seed. It's the same way in the
kingdom of God. Everything comes from the Word of God!

CRAZY FARMER

Now, that's a strong statement, but do you really believe it?
Are you trying to receive a miracle from God? Have you taken
the seed of God's Word—the promises that give you faith for
receiving that miracle—and planted them in your heart?

Are you trying to believe God for healing? Have you taken
the Scriptures, meditated on them, and planted the seed in
your heart? Or are you running to someone else and asking
them to pray for you? Are you just calling out to God and
pleading, "Oh Lord, please heal me!" and then wondering why
you aren't seeing the results?

Please don't take offense. I'm trying to help you, and this is
important. Wouldn't it be silly for a farmer to go out into their
field and wonder why they didn't have a harvest of corn growing up in their pasture when they never planted seeds? You'd
think they were crazy, wouldn't you?

It's the same in the spiritual realm. People ask, "Why hasn't
my crop grown up?"

"Have you planted any seed?"

"No."

If you want a harvest, you need to plant some seed. If you want healing to manifest in your life, you need to take God's promises and sow them into your heart. Don't just pray and ask for healing. Don't just run to someone else and ask them to pray for you to get healed. Take the Word of God that promises you His healing power and meditate on it. If you'll plant the seed, then you'll get a crop. If you don't plant the seed, then you won't get a crop.

SPITTING IN THE WIND

"Oh yeah, I believe in the importance of God's Word." Well, are you asking God to do something in your life that you honestly don't even know the Word promises?

People have come up to me by the hundreds, saying, "Could you pray for me?"

I'll ask, "What scripture are you standing on? What are you believing God for?"

They answer, "Well, I think the Bible says somewhere that..." and they'll try to quote something they haven't even read for themselves. They just heard it in passing. It's something they vaguely have in their minds, but they can't go to the Word of God and find it. They haven't personally taken the seed and meditated on it.

How do you plant the seed of God's Word in your heart? It's not like you just read it one time and that's it. You have to meditate on the Word of God until it releases its power, germinates, and begins to release its life. I can guarantee you that if you take a scripture that is promising you some result from God's Word and you meditate on it until it begins to release its life in *your* life, you'll be able to say what that scripture says.

Personally, I believe it's beneficial to even know the chapter and verse, because that helps you to go back and meditate on it. But I'm not going to say that you have to know the chapter and verse. Yet when you say something like, "Well, I believe the Bible says somewhere . . ." and then you just attempt to quote a scripture, you're spitting in the wind. You don't know the Word of God. You haven't meditated and put God's Word in your heart.

PERPLEXED

Are you someone who says, "Oh yes, I believe in the Word of God, and I believe that you have to really know God's Word," but when someone asks about God's promises, you don't know where in the Bible His promises are? Then you don't have a clue. Now, I'm not trying to be mean to you. Truly, I'm trying to help you. But I'm telling you, you don't know the Word of God.

You're doing the same thing as a farmer who wonders why his ground hasn't brought forth a crop, and yet he never planted seeds.

Many people say, "Oh yes, I believe in the Word. I believe the Word says this and that." But do they believe it to the point that it has caused them to meditate in it and study it? Lots of people were taught from the time they were a child that the Bible is God's Word. So, they'll stand up and fight for that. And yet they don't live like it's truly God's Word.

If this is really God speaking to you, and His Word is like a seed (Mark 4:14), then you must take His Word and plant it into your heart and life. But if you haven't meditated in the Word day and night (Josh. 1:8 and Ps. 1:2), if you aren't studying the Word, and if you don't know what it says, then don't be confused or surprised if you don't get the right results.

This is so simple, you have to have somebody help you to misunderstand it. If you're missing what I'm saying here, your elevator doesn't go all the way up to the top floor. This is just simple, foundational truth. You might be saying, "Let's move on. Let's go on to something greater," but until you live this truth, applying it to your everyday life, you don't really understand it yet.

Pastor, What's Wrong?

A man went one Sunday and auditioned at a certain church to become their new pastor. He preached a message from John 3:16. Everybody liked it, so they voted him in to the pastorate. When he came, his very first sermon as the new pastor was on John 3:16. The people thought this was unusual. They thought, *Somehow or another, he must have forgotten.* So, they didn't say anything. Then the next Sunday, his message was on

John 3:16 again. This really began to concern the folks. They started talking among themselves, but no one said anything to the pastor.

The third and fourth Sundays he was there, he also preached on—you guessed it—John 3:16. By now, the people were really concerned, so the deacons got together and approached him, saying, "Pastor, we don't know what's wrong, but you act like you don't remember. You've preached John 3:16 four times in a row. Don't you know anything else? We were expecting you to preach something new."

His response was, "When you start living what John 3:16 says, then I'll preach something different."

If that were the way we preached our messages, we wouldn't have to preach very many messages. Why? Because many people listen to the Word, but they never go out and do it.

God's Word is like a seed. You can sit there and say, "Oh yes, I believe in the importance of God's Word." But have you taken it and planted it in your heart? Are you asking God to perform a miracle in your life, yet you haven't sown the seed of that miracle in your heart? If you are, then you don't yet believe this truth. You might say, "Oh yes, I believe that the Word of God is essential for a Christian." But if you aren't meditating in it, studying the Word, basing your life on it—if you can't even quote the scripture that would give you the promise of what God said about your need—then you don't yet believe in the Word of God. You don't believe in it to the point that it's going to produce. And that's like a person who says, "I believe I have to plant that seed before I get my crop," but they never plant it.

So, don't be surprised if you don't get a crop. This is what Jesus was talking about.

Chapter 4

CAN'T BEAT GOD'S SYSTEM

When Jesus taught in Mark 4 that God's Word is like a seed, He wasn't trying to teach us how to be farmers. He was revealing that the natural seed has to be planted before we get a crop. And this is the same for the spiritual realm; we have to plant God's Word in our hearts before we receive from God. God's Word is like a spiritual seed.

First Peter 1:23 confirms this, saying,

> *Being born again, not of corruptible seed, but of incorruptible, by the word of God, which liveth and abideth for ever.*

The Greek word translated as *"seed"* in this verse is the word *spora*. This is talking about how plants proliferate through spores. The Greek word *spora* is akin to the Greek word *sperma*, which is where we get our English word *sperm*. This describes seed in the sense of a man sowing seed into a woman's womb and having a child. The Word of God is like that. In the same way a woman cannot have a child without the seed of a man, you cannot get the results from God that you desire without the Word of God being planted inside of you. In a sense, you must be impregnated with God's Word.

"Oh Andrew, I don't believe that. I believe that you can just cry out to God, and He will move in your life. You don't have to know the Word of God."

Well, I admit God loves us so much that He is willing and wanting to move in our lives. And for those who ignore His Word and don't know what it says, when they get into a crisis situation, they can cry out to Him for help and run to a messenger of God for prayer. God moves through other people. And yes, it is possible for you to receive an answer from God through somebody else's faith, through their intercession. God will use other people. It's like a surrogate birth. Things like that do happen.

EVERY MEMBER SUPPLIES

But if you draw from that the conclusion that you don't really have to know God's Word to be able to receive, that's untrue. Somebody else had to know God's Word. Somebody else had to take the seed of God's Word and plant it in their heart to give them the power and the anointing to be able to minister to and help you. But God did not intend that every time you have a need, you have to run to somebody and let them, through their faith, help you receive from Him. God meant for you to be able to receive directly from Him yourself.

Now, I am a minister, so I'm not against ministers. Ministry leaders are given to the church to help you.

> *And* [God] *gave some, apostles; and some, prophets; and some, evangelists; and some, pastors and teachers; For the perfecting of the saints, for the work of the ministry, for the edifying of the body of Christ.*
>
> **Ephesians 4:11-12, brackets added**

The Lord was saying here that He gave five types of leaders—apostles, prophets, evangelists, pastors, and teachers—so that through their ministry, they can help perfect and mature the saints. By doing so, the saints can then do the work of the ministry and edify, or build up, the body of Christ. Just keep on reading, and you'll see in verse 16 how every member supplies something and increases the body.

> *From whom the whole body fitly joined together and compacted by that which every joint supplieth, according to the effectual working in the measure of every part, maketh increase of the body unto the edifying of itself in love.*
>
> **Ephesians 4:16**

In context, this passage isn't talking about these ministry leaders—the pastor, the clergy, etc.—doing all of your believing for you. It's also not saying that you can run to them for prayer and get everything through them. They are there to help you and to teach you the Word of God. That way, you can start taking God's Word for yourself, letting it take root on the inside of you, and then you can receive your miracle directly from God.

NOT NORMAL PROCEDURE

Yes, it's true that you can bootleg a miracle, in a sense, off somebody else's faith. But that's not intended to be a normal procedure. That isn't supposed to be the normal Christian life.

It's just like if you were in a storm, and your house had been built on the sand (Matt. 7:26). Because it wasn't founded on God's Word, your house would collapse. You might run next door and step inside your neighbor's house to weather the storm. But you aren't supposed to then live with your neighbor and live off their faith. You're supposed to go back, dig down, and lay a sure foundation for your house upon the bedrock of God's Word (Matt. 7:24). Then once you're established, you'll be able to withstand the next storm on your own (Matt. 7:25).

I'm not saying that you don't ever get help from somebody else. We all need help from time to time. But I am saying that unless you accept this truth—that you cannot receive a blessing or a miracle from God without the Word of God in your life any more than a woman can have a child without the seed of a man—you're going to fail as a Christian. You could say, "Oh no, I don't believe I have to really know the Word of God. I'll just go to somebody else and let them pray for me." It might work once. It might work twice. You might be able to do that on a few occasions, but if that's your attitude, you're going to fail as a Christian.

You may still go to heaven. I'm not saying that you'll lose your salvation. I'm just pointing out that you'll probably get there quicker because you won't know how to receive your healing from God. By not knowing the Word for yourself, you won't know how to deal with the stress, disappointments, and hurts in this life.

Everything God does, He does through His Word. That's a simple statement, but it's one that most people don't believe. They certainly don't believe it to the degree that they act on it, taking God's Word and meditating in it.

IT TAKES TIME TO SOW

The Lord used a natural illustration on how the kingdom of God works, because social systems can be beat. You can beat some social systems that man has devised—school, courts, etc.—but you can't beat a natural system like planting a seed in the ground in order to produce the desired crop.

Think about it. There was probably a time when you goofed off in school. You didn't really study or do your homework like you should. You waited until the night before the exam and then started popping caffeine pills or drinking coffee. You stayed up late cramming for the final, and you learned the material well enough to be able to put an answer down and pass the test. But now, years later, there's no way you could pass that same test. It's because you didn't really learn the material. You just had it in your short-term memory so you could pass the exam. In a sense, you beat the system. You broke the system. It didn't work properly. You may have been able to earn a passing grade, but you didn't get what you needed from that educational system.

You can beat a manmade system, like our schools, by cramming for a test and passing a final, but you can't do that with a natural system. You can't just ignore the right time to sow a seed, neglecting to cultivate it with water and fertilizer, and expect to get a crop. You can't just goof off for months, wait until the night before your neighbor harvests their crop, go out and work frantically to plant seed in the ground, and wind up getting your harvest the next day too. It doesn't work that way. You can't beat a natural system. That's why the Lord used a natural system to teach this truth about how the kingdom works. You can't cheat sowing a seed and reaping a harvest. You miss the right time to sow, and I don't care what you do and how much effort you put into it the night before a harvest is due, you're not going to get a crop.

It's the same way in the spiritual realm. You might be able to beat a social system, but in the spiritual realm, you can't just goof off—not seek God and not plant the Word into your life—but get good results. You can't just sow worry, fear, and unforgiveness instead, and then come into a situation where you need a miracle and receive it. You can't just forget everything and then fast for one day, pray, cry out to God, and get your miracle. If you're in that situation, you're going to have to go to another person who has been faithfully taking God's Word, sowing it into their life, and let them help you, using their faith and their anointing, to get your answer. You aren't going to receive a supernatural crop overnight. It takes time to sow God's Word into your life!

REVOLUTIONARY

God's Word is like a seed. If you want a crop, you have to plant a seed. If you want God's best in your life, you have to know God's Word. And if you haven't put that importance on God's Word yet, then you haven't laid the right foundation.

This truth is revolutionary. It's how God's kingdom works. This could change your life!

Chapter 5

GREAT FAITH

G od's Word is the foundation of everything in our Christian
lives. It's so important that we base our faith on the Word.

*And when Jesus was entered into Capernaum,
there came unto him a centurion, beseeching him,
And saying, Lord, my servant lieth at home sick
of the palsy, grievously tormented. And Jesus saith
unto him, I will come and heal him. The centurion
answered and said, Lord, I am not worthy that
thou shouldest come under my roof: but speak the
word only, and my servant shall be healed. For I
am a man under authority, having soldiers under
me: and I say to this man, Go, and he goeth; and to
another, Come, and he cometh; and to my servant,
Do this, and he doeth it. When Jesus heard it, he
marvelled, and said to them that followed, Verily*

*I say unto you, I have not found so great faith, no,
not in Israel.*

Matthew 8:5-10

Then the Lord went on, in verses 11 and 12, about how
Gentiles would come to Him exhibiting greater faith than the
nation of Israel did. Of course, this infuriated the Jews when
He said this.

This man came to Jesus and requested that He perform a
miracle for him by healing his servant who was dying of a
fever. Christ answered and said that He would come to this
man's home and heal his servant. But the centurion said that
he didn't need Jesus to come to his house. Instead, the centurion said, *"Speak the word only, and my servant shall be healed"*
(Matt. 8:8).

JESUS MARVELED

This was a centurion—a ranking Roman officer who had
about a hundred Roman soldiers under him. And he basically
said, "I know the power of words. If I tell my servant to do this,
he does it. If I say, 'Come here,' he comes. Whatever I say gets
carried out." This man recognized the authority and power that
are in God's words. After all, he told Jesus to speak the Word
only and it would be done. And when Jesus heard this, He
marveled (Matt. 8:10).

There are only two times in Scripture when Jesus marveled:
one is here, at the centurion's great faith, and the other is in

Mark 6, when He marveled at people's unbelief. Jesus was amazed that a man could operate in this strong of a faith. It wasn't typical. It wasn't what the Lord saw in most people. And He was amazed that even His disciples could be so full of unbelief after spending so much time with Him.

Notice how Jesus marveled and then said to the people who followed Him, *"Verily I say unto you, I have not found so great faith, no, not in Israel"* (Matt. 8:10).

What made this man's faith great? It was because his faith was in the Word alone. He didn't need Jesus to come and wave His hand over the servant. He didn't need the Lord to enter into his house and do something.

Many people today use all kinds of things to motivate and, in a sense, psych themselves into believing. I'm not saying that those things shouldn't be used, because God is very intent on trying to get His blessings and His power to people. I believe He uses a lot of things that aren't His first or best choice. But I can tell you from this passage of Scripture what is God's best. The type of faith He respects the most is the kind that goes to His Word, takes what He says, and believes His Word more than anything else. That's awesome!

BE NOT FAITHLESS

Contrast this type of faith with the faith of one of Jesus's disciples:

> *But Thomas, one of the twelve, called Didymus, was not with them when Jesus came. The other disciples therefore said unto him, We have seen the Lord. But he said unto them, Except I shall see in his hands the print of the nails, and put my finger into the print of the nails, and thrust my hand into his side, I will not believe.*

John 20:24-25

Jesus had been raised from the dead. He appeared to some of His disciples after His resurrection, but Thomas wasn't present with them. He declared that unless he could see Him, stick his finger in the print of His nails, and thrust his hand into His side, he would not believe.

> *And after eight days again his disciples were within, and Thomas with them: then came Jesus, the doors being shut, and stood in the midst, and said, Peace be unto you. Then saith he to Thomas, Reach hither thy finger, and behold my hands; and reach hither thy hand, and thrust it into my side: and be not faithless, but believing.*

John 20:26-27

Nobody told Jesus what Thomas had said. Christ wasn't present when Thomas said those things, and none of the other disciples had encountered the Lord between His first appearance and the second. Yet when Jesus walked into the room,

He immediately turned to Thomas and told him to put his finger into the nail prints in His hands and to thrust his hand into His side. In other words, it showed that He was God and all-knowing. Jesus knew exactly what Thomas had spoken, and He offered him the proof that he said he required.

PSYCHED INTO BELIEVING

So, what did Thomas do? *"And Thomas answered and said unto him, My Lord and my God"* (John 20:28).

There is no indication that Thomas actually touched Jesus. But when he saw the Lord and realized that Jesus knew exactly what he had been thinking and what he had said, that was proof enough. He fell down on his face, declaring, *"My Lord and my God"* (John 20:28).

> *And Jesus saith unto him, Thomas, because thou hast seen me, thou hast believed: blessed are they that have not seen, and yet have believed.*
>
> **John 20:29**

In a sense, Jesus was saying, "Thomas, you're blessed because you fell down, acknowledging and believing that I was resurrected from the dead. But there's a greater blessing on those who have believed without seeing."

In other words, there is a greater blessing on those who believe the Word and who believe because of the promises.

There is a greater anointing on those people's lives than on others who believe because they have seen, it's been proven to them, or they've been psyched into believing God.

Two Sections

There are things that can be done that will, in a sense, manipulate people into a place of believing. A friend of mine used to travel with a famous healing evangelist named Jack Coe. Jack saw some great miracles. I actually met his son once, over in France, and he confirmed some of the miracles. For instance, a woman at one of his meetings had a big cancerous growth on her face. Jack just put his hand on it, and it appeared like he was massaging it. But Jack was actually digging his fingernails beneath the growth. He ripped that growth off this woman's face, and blood spurted everywhere. Then he turned around and slapped her upside the face. When he did, instantly her flesh grew over the wound. It was a miraculous healing!

Jack did see some great miracles, but this friend of mine, who used to travel with him for a time, got so mad because Jack would sometimes deceive people. This was back in the 1950s when there were tent meetings and people would travel long distances to be there. Many invalids came to the services, and my friend's job was to go to the people who were on stretchers, crutches, and wheelchairs and test them to see if they could get up and go to one of the portable toilets. The people who were on stretchers, crutches, and wheelchairs who could get up and move—even though they had problems—would be put at the front of the tent. But those who couldn't get up would be put at the back of the tent. So, my friend was in charge of separating them into these two sections.

Jack would get up, preach on healing, and then jump off the stage and run down to the invalid section at the front of the tent. The people in the crowd didn't know (but my friend knew) that the people in that section could all stand up and shuffle. They had problems, but they could all get up and go relieve themselves. Well, Jack would take these people's crutches away from them, and they would start moving and shuffling. And the crowd would just go bananas, thinking that these people were totally healed. Of course, nothing had really happened to them. But Jack would take their stretchers and wheelchairs and put them on the stage, talking about how they were healed.

My friend saw this, took offense, and decided to leave, vowing that he wouldn't come back because Jack was a crook.

SUBMIT YOURSELF AND SERVE

As my friend was driving out of town, the Lord spoke to him, asking, "But what does Jack do after he ministers to that invalid section in the front?"

"Well, he goes to the back of the tent and sees two or three hundred people, who are totally paralyzed, healed per night."

And the Lord told my friend, "Go back, submit yourself, and just serve this guy."

People have a natural type of unbelief. They're just naturally skeptical, and there are things that can be done to help them get over it. Now, I'm not saying that's the way it should be done. I don't believe that's the way Jesus would have done it. But nonetheless, it illustrates how people can be manipulated toward faith. Things can be said and done that will increase and spark faith on the inside of them, which then helps them to receive.

That's not the highest form of faith. And that shouldn't be the level we sink to. God wants us to be like the centurion who said, *"Speak the word only, and my servant shall be healed"* (Matt. 8:8). That's the great faith Jesus marveled at.

Chapter 6

GOD'S BEST

The highest form of faith comes from just believing God's Word alone (Matt. 8:10) and not needing something else to quicken your faith. Jack Coe would minister to people in the front of the tent first, the ones who looked like they were crippled but really weren't, or were crippled to a degree but could still move. Then, once the crowd's faith had risen, he would go to the back of the tent and minister to those who were totally paralyzed, and he would see them healed. This is an example of how things can be done to quicken people's faith.

Jack used this technique to create an atmosphere of faith where he could go back and minister to the people who were totally paralyzed and see them healed. Even though I don't believe that this is God's best, there is some validity for doing this.

In my meetings, I go out of my way not to use any hype or try psych people up. I just try to get them to trust the Word and believe God. I reach for a purity of faith like the centurion had. But the Lord showed me that most people aren't to that level yet. There are some folks who have sincere, desperate needs in their lives. And because I go out of my way not to do anything to lead people into some kind of momentary faith, there are people I choose not to minister to.

AN ATMOSPHERE OF FAITH

I went to a famous evangelist's meeting who was known for the supernatural things that regularly happened in his services. I don't doubt that God does the miraculous. I believe it, and I've seen it. But I wanted to find out if there was anything that this man did to help create this atmosphere for miracles.

Other than during an offering, he didn't actually teach the Word for the first four or five meetings. Now, he did later. But for the first four or five services, he brought hundreds of people with him whose lives had been changed in his meetings. He would have these people start giving testimonies. They would get up and talk about the miraculous things that God had done. Through this, this man created an atmosphere of faith. He built people's expectancy to such a high level that anybody could have stood up there and seen miracles happen because the people's expectancy had been brought to such a high place by all the testimonies.

When I perceived what he was doing—in a sense, manipulating the crowds—my first reaction was to discredit that. But when I pondered on how he was getting all these people together into an atmosphere of faith, I realized that so many people just live submerged in an atmosphere of unbelief. They really do need something to jump-start them and get them moving toward the Lord and His Word in faith.

I don't want to do things that discourage people's faith. My aim and goal is for them to receive. So, when I minister in a prayer line and perceive when the anointing of God flows through my hands into a person, I'll say something to them. It used to be that I'd perceive it but wouldn't say anything about it. I'd know that God was healing them and I'd say, "Praise God. Thank You, Jesus," and go on.

Just like Jesus did when He perceived virtue flowing out of His robe and into this woman who was healed (Mark 5:30), I've learned to stop and say something to the person I'm ministering to when I feel the anointing of God. I'll say, "That's the anointing of God flowing into your body." Instead of just ignoring it and moving on like I used to do, my pausing and saying something to the person helps quicken their faith.

THE LORD MET HIM

Now, people shouldn't put their faith in what I feel or what I say. The ultimate is to be like the centurion with great faith who said, *"Speak the word only, and my servant shall be healed"* (Matt. 8:8). That's what I try to encourage. Our whole ministry is about the integrity of God's Word. That has to be the foundation. However, until people get there, they need help. Sometimes encouraging them a little helps them to receive the miracle they need. That little jump-start to their faith gets them to where they can believe the Word of God and receive.

There are two different ways of receiving from God. One of the ways is to be like Thomas, the disciple of Jesus who said, "I'm not going to believe unless I can see it, feel it, or touch it. Unless there's some kind of physical, carnal proof that comes across my path to quicken my faith, I won't believe" (John 20:25). Do you know what? The Lord met Thomas where he was. He said, "All right, Thomas. Put your finger into the print of the nails. Put your hand into My side. Don't be faithless, but believing." The Lord met him at his inferior, immature level of faith.

But when Thomas fell down and declared "My Lord, my God," Jesus didn't respond by saying, "Well, Thomas, you're awesome. This is the way it's supposed to be." Really, the Lord said, "Thomas, you've seen and therefore you believe."

The other way of receiving from God is to believe *without* seeing, to believe without somehow or another being manipulated or encouraged (John 20:29). God was saying that there's a greater blessing on the person who just takes God's Word and believes it without needing to have three dreams, two prophecies, and a vision to confirm what He says.

This truth changed my life! As a boy, I was raised in the Baptist church. Back then, they strongly preached salvation. But other than the miracle of the new birth, they didn't really say much. They didn't necessarily teach against miracles, but they certainly didn't teach for them either.

So then faith cometh by hearing, and hearing by the word of God.

Romans 10:17

The absence of such teaching led us all to believe that God didn't do miracles today. The church just taught a person how to get saved, and that was basically it.

BAPTISM OF THE HOLY SPIRIT

When I came into the baptism of the Holy Spirit, I began to recognize that miracles didn't pass away and that God is still doing supernatural things on the earth today. I started hearing testimonies of people who saw angels, received visions, and had dreams. All of it was scriptural. All of it was in the Bible.

When I began to realize that these things were possible, I started craving them. I prayed, "Oh God, show me an angel. Oh God, let fire come down and burn in my hands when I pray for people." I was praying for all these physical manifestations. Then the Lord spoke to me and said, "Andrew, if you keep pressing Me in this area, you can see visions and dreams. It's not evil or bad, but it's not My best. There's a greater anointing on a person who believes because of the promise of My Word alone and not because they see angels, visions, or dreams. That's My best."

That's when I changed my prayer to "God, I want Your best. I don't care if I ever see a vision or an angel." Do you know what? I've never seen an angel. I have never heard an audible voice. And yet God has spoken to me supernaturally through the Word.

People have come up to me at my meetings and reported that they've seen angels standing on either side of me. Many miracles have happened!

In Charlotte, North Carolina, the Lord told me one time that He was going to show me how angels were supernaturally at work in my meetings. I didn't tell anyone, but I was expecting to hear some testimonies about it. Over the course of the week's meetings, four or five things occurred.

THE HIGHEST FORM OF FAITH

One of them was when I called out a healing and a young man came forward. The power of God hit him, and he fell on the ground. When he got up, we asked him to give a testimony. He said, "When you called that out, somebody put their hand on my shoulder. It was so real, but when I turned around and looked, no actual person was there." This was the rebellious son of a woman who had come to my meeting. This guy didn't want to be there. He didn't believe in any of this, yet he physically felt someone touch him. He said, "I turned around, I saw an angel, God spoke to me, and I came forward."

Things like that happen. I'm aware that they exist. I believe it. I've never seen it personally, yet I believe. And the Lord showed me that this is the highest form of faith—to simply take the promise of God's Word and believe it.

What about you? Maybe you believe in the supernatural power of God. Maybe you know some of the promises, but the truth is, God's Word isn't enough for you. You have to have two angels, three visions, and four goose bumps before you'd believe anything. If that's where you are, God will meet you there as much as He can, but it's not going to be His best. God's best is for you to become like the centurion and say, "Lord, I don't need You to touch me. I don't need to see You. I don't need anything except Your Word" (Matt. 8:8).

The good news is, God has given you lots of promises in His Word. You have so many promises! If you could just move into that realm of faith, a great and pure faith, to where God's Word becomes as real to you as something you can see, taste, hear, smell, or feel, it'll cause you to receive greater blessings.

That's what I want. I'm not after His second best or third best. My aim and goal is God's best—believing His Word alone. Hallelujah!

Chapter 7

SOWING AND REAPING

At Charis Bible College, we don't teach philosophy, theory, or mere experience. We teach the Word of God and use experience, or anything else, only as it lines up with the Bible. God's Word is our sure foundation.

The kingdom of God works by sowing and reaping (Gal. 6:7-8). And you can only reap what you sow. That's why it's important to take God's Word and meditate on it until it releases its life and power into your life.

I've met many Christians who were confused, bitter, and angry—even at God! They were upset about why things hadn't worked out in their lives. Yet they hadn't taken God's Word like a seed and planted it in their hearts. So, their grievances with the Lord were completely unjustified.

If you don't know God's Word better than you know what's going on in the stock market, better than you know what's happening in the headlines, better than you know the stats for your favorite sports team—better than all these physical, natural things—then don't be surprised if you get more natural results than spiritual results. That's just how the kingdom works.

NO SEED, NO CROP

> *And he said, So is the kingdom of God, as if a man should cast seed into the ground; And should sleep, and rise night and day, and the seed should spring and grow up, he knoweth not how. For the earth bringeth forth fruit of herself; first the blade, then the ear, after that the full corn in the ear. But when the fruit is brought forth, immediately he putteth in the sickle, because the harvest is come.*

Mark 4:26-29

The people Jesus taught were very familiar with agriculture. They didn't just go to the store and buy vegetables. Most of them planted their own crops. They were well acquainted with the realities of farming. The Lord used these natural truths about gardening, or sowing and reaping, to illustrate spiritual truths.

God's Word is like a seed (Mark 4:14). And that seed needs to be planted in our hearts. Our hearts are the ground that the seed, or God's Word, springs up and grows in. This is how His kingdom is released into our lives. No seed, no crop. No Word, no miracle. This is true in the natural realm, and it's true in the spiritual realm.

> *And* [the man] *should sleep, and rise night and day, and the seed should spring and grow up, he knoweth not how.*
>
> **Mark 4:27, brackets added**

Mark 4:27 is saying that the man plants the seed, he sleeps and rises night and day, and then the seed springs forth and grows up of its own, yet he doesn't know how. Do you know what this is saying? It's saying that once a seed is planted, there is a time element involved for the seed to be able to germinate and produce.

LEAVE IT THERE

Let's say you took a seed and planted it in the ground. What would happen if you came back the next morning and dug it up? Would anything have happened? Well, in one day's time, nothing would have happened.

So, let's say you replant it, and the next day you dig it up again to look at it. This time you leave the seed out for three or four days before replanting it again. Then you go back and dig it up again a day or two later. This time you leave it out for a week before replanting it. Did you know that this seed will never release its power?

The way God created a seed to work is by you putting it in the ground and leaving it there. You can't be digging it up every hour to see if something is happening. Instead, you must leave it there by faith and believe it will produce because God said it would.

It's the same way with God's Word. Let's say you've accepted the challenge to make God's Word a higher priority. So, you go and spend five minutes in the Word, read a few things, and have a few positive thoughts. Then you go out to your job and just violate everything you've read by the way you talk, walk, and live. The next morning, you go back and spend five or ten minutes in the Word again, but you still go out and live your day totally contrary to those scriptures you've read. Then you skip the Word for four or five days, until it's time for church. You attend the Sunday service and listen to the preacher. God speaks to you through the message, and because of it, you start getting excited. But then you just leave it alone for the next week or so.

Can you see what you're doing? You're just like the person who plants a seed in the ground but then uproots it to look at it. And because you can't perceive that anything's happening, you lose your faith. No, you have to leave the seed of the Word in your heart and let it grow. That's how the Word of God works.

Five minutes in the Word is not going to counterbalance sixteen hours of unbelief per day. You have to take God's Word and meditate on it. Take a truth from God's Word and think about it. You might read something during your devotional time in the morning, and God speaks to you about it. Your attitude ought to be, "Lord, please help me to remember this throughout today. I'm going to let this truth that You've spoken to me live on the inside of me. I want it to influence the way I think and act."

DUG UP

Say, for instance, that you read, *"Take therefore no thought for the morrow: for the morrow shall take thought for the things of itself"* (Matt. 6:34). Don't worry about what you're going to eat, where you're going to sleep, or how you're going to be clothed (Matt. 6:25-34). *"But seek ye first the kingdom of God, and his righteousness; and all these things shall be added unto you"* (Matt. 6:33). You read these verses in your morning devotional time, but then you go out during the day and something comes up. It looks like you won't have enough money to pay your bills, they're going to repossess your car, etc. Well, are you going to just uproot that Word you've heard and start worrying and taking cares? Or are you going to do what the Word says?

Pray, "Father, I just read Matthew 6:25-34 today. You said not to take thought for these things. You said to seek first Your kingdom and Your righteousness, and You would add all these things to me. I'm going to trust You. I'm going to let Your Word work in my life!"

You may have to resist some fears and other contrary thoughts, but fight them off. Deal with them, and let God's Word dwell richly in your heart (Col. 3:16). Base your thought life and your actions on what God's Word says instead of what the banker, your neighbor, or the news has to say. If you start doing that, then you'll let that Word stay on the inside of you.

When something happens that's contrary to what you've read in the Word and you say, "I don't know where my next meal is coming from, we're going to lose our house, the car is going to be repossessed, nothing's working . . ." and you begin thinking, speaking, and acting contrary to what you've read, then you've just dug up the seed of the Word. That seed is not rooted, and it's not staying in your heart. You let the cares of this life and other things choke it and steal it from you (Mark 4:16-19). That Word won't profit you unless you start letting it control your thoughts, your emotions, and your actions.

I pray that you're getting what I'm saying. These are powerful, practical truths! I know you might want something deeper, but this is what you need. If you take God's Word and let it stay in your heart, it'll be like a seed that you plant in the ground. Let it remain there. It may take a week, a month, or more before you even start seeing a little sprout come up, but you have to give it time to work. There is a time of sowing and reaping.

A LIFESTYLE

It's the same way with the Word of God. Have you said, "I think I'm going to try this," and then spent five minutes in the

Word, expecting to see your life instantly change? Or maybe if you aren't absolutely healed, if your marriage isn't restored, or if things don't improve in the next ten minutes, you just dig up the seed of the Word and conclude, "Well, it didn't work."

That is absolutely as stupid as a person who plants a seed in the ground for five minutes and wonders why they didn't get a full stalk of corn. That's not the way it works. You can't dig up your seed, look at it, put it back in the ground, and then dig it up, look at it, and put it back in the ground, and keep doing that. No, you just have to leave it there and allow it time to germinate.

You can't just spend five minutes in the Word, pray a prayer, and, if your life doesn't instantly smooth out and everything begin to work, say, "Well, the Word didn't produce." No, you only gave it five minutes in the soil. You only left it in your heart for a brief period of time.

This has to be a lifestyle. You have to get to where you start believing God's Word. Day and night, you rise and live, letting God's Word begin to control you. And over a period of time, it'll be just like it says in Mark 4:27: you'll sleep, and rise night and day, and the seed will spring and grow up, though you know not how.

Chapter 8

HOW DO I CHANGE?

And [he] *should sleep, and rise night and day, and the seed should spring and grow up, he knoweth not how.*

Mark 4:27, brackets added

This verse says that the seed grows up on its own, and he doesn't understand how. Isn't that awesome?

I don't understand how this works, but it does. I can personally testify to you that this truly works. If you would just put God's Word in your heart by reading it, meditating on it, thinking about it, and trying to conform your emotions, thoughts, and actions to it, the seed will grow up on its own. I don't know how it does that, but change comes.

In fact, my teaching entitled *Effortless Change* deals with this truth in greater detail than I'm able to do here. And I know that this idea of change being effortless sounds like an oxymoron. How can a person experience effortless change? For most people, change comes with great difficulty and effort, especially in the Christian life. Christians often view change as involving strenuous labor. However, that's because they aren't going about it God's way.

God's method of change, maturity, growth, and victory in your life involves taking the Word of God, which is the seed of all change, and sowing it in your heart consistently over a period of time. And when you follow God's method, making it your very lifestyle, the Word just produces change, and you don't know how it happens.

Beginning to Panic

While listening to another minister share during a recording of a conference, I heard this man speak about some of the different hardships and hiccups he'd been through. It just made me feel so blessed! I've avoided a lot of the problems that many people go through. Now, I'm not saying this to my credit. It wasn't because of me or something great I had done. It's just God! By placing an importance on God's Word, knowing Him, and learning what His Word says, God has changed my life effortlessly.

If I were to go back and try to relive the last fifty years on my own wisdom, I wouldn't have a chance of doing things as well as they have been done. It's not because I figured this stuff out. It's because I've stayed in relationship with God, and I've stayed in His Word. God's Word has changed my attitude, my emotions, and my thoughts. That's how this works.

When I first got turned on to the Lord, I had a miraculous encounter with Him on March 23, 1968. I came to experience His love. It was an emotional experience that revolutionized my life and turned me right side up. But the emotion could not have carried me through these past fifty years. The emotion jump-started me and dramatically got my attention, but what really changed my life was God's Word.

After the emotion of that experience began to wane, and even though I'd been reading and studying the Word, I realized that I hadn't really made the Word as important as it should have been. I was eighteen or nineteen years old and still living at home with my mother. I'd been reading the Bible, so it was lying open on the bed one day as I knelt down and prayed. I said, "Oh God, I feel like the emotion of what You've done in my life is wearing off." Beginning to panic, I said, "Lord, I don't want to lose this. I don't want to lose my love for You!" I knew that God had great things in store for my life, but I had no idea how to get there from where I was. So, I asked Him, "Lord, how do I get there from here?" It looked like such a huge distance to cover. "God, what do I do? How do I do this? How do I retain these things?"

When I opened my eyes, which had been closed, it was like—*boom*—there was the Bible. In my heart, I heard the Lord say, *If you will just put the importance and priority on knowing My Word, studying My Word, and meditating in My*

Word, then My Word will do everything that you need. It wasn't an audible voice, but rather something I just heard on the inside of me. Yet I took it just as if God had spoken it to me in an audible voice.

HUNGER

So, I began to spend as many as sixteen and sometimes twenty hours a day just reading and reading, studying and studying, meditating and meditating, and trying to live by the Word. Here I am, five decades later, and I can truthfully tell you that God's Word has taught me and has done everything that I've needed.

You might be feeling desperate right now, just like I was. You're not sure how to get from where you are to where you believe God wants to you be, and it seems like it's such a major effort. You're asking, "How do I change? How do I do this?" I'm giving you my personal testimony. It's God's Word! Just like Mark 4:27 says, it just springs and grows up of itself. You don't have to understand it.

I don't understand it. I couldn't go back and outline my life and tell you why all of these things work. However, I can tell you one key thing: I have spent fifty years seeking God and meditating in His Word day and night. Because of my schedule now, I don't spend as much time as I used to in the Word, but I'm still meditating on it constantly. I listen to audio teachings whenever I can. I still have a hunger just to read God's Word.

A while back I spent one entire day, maybe ten hours or more, just sitting and reading God's Word. I had some other things I wanted to do, but I just got so excited reading the Word that I couldn't put it down. Here I am, fifty years later, and I'm still doing it. I've read these things hundreds, even thousands, of times. I feel like the prophet who declared, "God's Word burns on the inside of me!" (Jer. 20:9). It excites me.

If I start getting discouraged, worried, or full of care about something, all I have to do is go to the scriptures that talk about the faithfulness of God and how He has provided for me. I read them, and it's just like fire. It comes in and burns up all the worry, care, and frustration.

IT'S WORKING

You might be thinking, *You're weird, Andrew. This is weird. I don't understand what you're talking about. The Word of God doesn't burn on the inside of me.* Well, I'm telling you that it can, and it should. If it doesn't, it's not because God doesn't want it to be that way for you, but because you haven't placed the proper priority and importance on it yet.

The Holy Spirit is a wonderful teacher, but you have to show up for class. You have to walk into the classroom, sit down, and pay attention to what He's saying. What good is it to have the Holy Spirit as your teacher if you never go to school? The Word of God is intended to be like fire shut up in your bones. It's supposed to bring forth change in your life. God created the Word, and that's what the Word is for.

Jesus appeared in His resurrection body and walked to Emmaus with two of His disciples, but they didn't recognize Him at first (Luke 24). Jesus expounded the Scriptures to them, and they finally realized who He was when He blessed the bread at supper. He vanished out of their sight, and they said, *"Did not our heart burn within us, while he talked with us by the way, and while he opened to us the scriptures?"* (Luke 24:32). That's the way it's supposed to be.

But the Word won't affect you like that or change you if it just sits on your coffee table. You can't lay the Bible on top of your head and receive fire, victory, faith, and power. You must read, meditate, and start conforming your thoughts and actions to it. You have to let the Word become the dominant force in your life. You can't just grab one of the little cards out of your Daily Bread box as you walk out the door—reading one verse a day, a week, or whatever—and think that you're in the Word. It's going to take some time. You're going to have to put some effort into it. But just as Mark 4:27 says, *"The seed should spring and grow up."* You don't know how, but it works. That's awesome! I enjoy that to this day, even though I still don't understand everything.

There are certain times when I just kind of hit a dead end. I try this, and pursue that, but nothing works. I seek the Lord and ask Him about it, but I may not even be sure how to pray. Do you know what I do in a situation like that? I just sit down with my Bible and start reading. I begin worshiping God, loving on Him, and asking Him to speak to me. It isn't long before the Lord says something to me that directly applies to my situation.

This is how God moves in my life. I know I'm not a perfect example, but it's working. And this is how it works for me. You might be saying, "I wish it would work for me the way you're describing." It can if you will give the same effort to it that I've given. You need to take God's Word, plant it in your heart, and let it stay there. Don't dig it up. If you live out God's Word by conforming your life to it, God's Word will work for you. The Word is never the problem. It's us not putting God's Word into our hearts that's the problem.

Chapter 9

UNDER THE
INFLUENCE

Just like a natural seed planted in the ground brings forth a crop, God has designed your heart to bring forth a harvest from the spiritual seed of His Word.

> *The seed should spring and grow up, he knoweth not how. For the earth bringeth forth fruit of herself; first the blade, then the ear, after that the full corn in the ear. But when the fruit is brought forth, immediately he putteth in the sickle, because the harvest is come.*

Mark 4:27-29

If you will let God's Word dwell in your heart on a consistent basis, your heart will automatically begin to change.

Your heart will bring forth fruit. It will begin releasing joy and love instead of fear, anger, and bitterness. Your heart will start releasing faith instead of doubt and unbelief. Your heart will interact with God's Word.

Most Christians don't believe this truth. If they did, they'd spend more time in the Word of God meditating and thinking about it. If they understood this principle and really believed it, they would invest more time in God's Word. That's all there is to it.

TIME

You can evaluate your commitment to the Word of God by how much time you devote to it. The true priority you place on God's Word is reflected by the amount of time you give to it.

Now, you might say, "Oh Andrew, I believe God's Word is foundational. It's very important, and we should give it priority in our lives."

Well then, let me ask you this: How much time do you spend actually reading and meditating on the Word of God? Many Christians would insist, "Oh yes, it's a priority in my life," but they couldn't prove it by their actions. They spend so very little time engaging their hearts with the Word.

I recognize that sometimes things happen, and we aren't always able to spend the time we would like to in the Word. When Jamie and I were evacuated from our house because of wildfires nearby, I was busy packing up and moving. During a time like that, a person just can't spend a lot of time sitting and reading the Bible. But those are exceptions.

DAILY FOOD

It's like eating food. Typically, we eat three times a day. Some people eat more than three times a day. But you know what? No one starves to death by missing a meal.

But what would happen if you only ate one meal a day, or even one meal a week? Would you be able to still maintain your health? You could skip a meal due to a stressful situation, but you can't make a habit of *not* eating and still be able to perform.

Well, in the same way, you need to take God's Word like you would your normal food and meditate, or chew, on it constantly. Now, something may come up where you aren't able to feed on it one day, but you aren't going to die. It's not like you're doomed to failure if you miss your Bible reading. However, I am saying that this needs to be the exception rather than the rule. You need to get to where you esteem God's Word more than your daily food.

That's how Job felt about it.

> *I have esteemed the words of his mouth more than my necessary food.*

> **Job 23:12**

Job valued God's Word more than his daily food. What if you adopted that as your attitude? What if you made this your daily practice? What could happen in, to, and through you if you fed on the Word that often? God has designed your heart to change under the influence of His Word.

HOW MUCH YOU GET

> *The heart is deceitful above all things, and desper-*
> *ately wicked: who can know it?*
>
> **Jeremiah 17:9**

If you take away God's Word and let your heart go on its own, it's going to start conceiving all kinds of sinful, evil things. You need to have the influence of God's Word on your heart. However, what's most important isn't how much you read, but how much you *get* from what you read that makes the difference.

> *For the earth bringeth forth fruit of herself; first*
> *the blade, then the ear, after that the full corn in*
> *the ear.*
>
> **Mark 4:28**

It's not about whether you read fifteen chapters a day. Rather, it's how much you *get* from the words that you read.

WHAT ARE YOU DOING?

I've had a Bible reading plan where I've read through the Bible on a regular basis. Now, this reading plan isn't all the Bible reading I do, but it is a consistent, systematic plan that I've tried to regularly follow.

During one season of my life when I was following this plan, I often prayed, "Father, I'm studying Your Word so that I can fellowship with You. Please give me revelation. Lord, speak to me through Your Word." Then I'd start my daily reading. One day as I read the first or second verse, my heart began interacting with the Word, and all these thoughts I'd never had started coming to me. I saw things I had never seen before, and I started receiving revelation from God. I literally found myself putting the Bible down, kicking back in my chair, and just meditating and thinking on what God was speaking to me. Good things were happening.

Then I caught myself and thought, *Man, this is only the second verse. I've got twenty-five more chapters to read!* Immediately I shut down my mind to those thoughts and went back to reading. As I was reading, I felt the Lord speak to me and say, "What are you doing?"

I answered, "Well, God, I'm reading the Word."

He asked, "Why are you reading the Word?"

I said, "I'm reading the Word so You can speak to me."

Then it just got quiet. God didn't say anything else. I got to thinking, *Well, what's all this about?* Then it dawned on me.

Here I was, asking the Lord to speak to me. So, He spoke to me on the second verse, and, in a sense, I told Him, "No, God, not now. Can't You tell that I'm reading the Word? How dare You interrupt my Bible study!"

HEAR FROM GOD

It sounds terrible, I know. But I'm just being honest with you. Have you done the same thing?

Have you read the Word in order to feel like you've got a feather in your cap, like you've done something that will make you satisfied with yourself? And did you forget that the purpose of reading the Word is to hear from God? Hey, if God starts speaking to you on the first word of the first sentence, then forget the rest of the Bible reading for the moment and let the Lord tell you what He wants to say.

The purpose of being in the Word is so that God can influence your heart. And if your heart is being changed through reading one verse, then just read that verse over and over and over again until your heart receives the full benefit from it.

Like it says in the Psalms, *"Selah."* (Pause and think about it.)

Chapter 10

AUTOMATICALLY

Look at Mark 4:28 again:

> *For the earth bringeth forth fruit of herself; first the blade, then the ear, after that the full corn in the ear.*

The Greek word translated *"of herself"* is *automatos*, which means "self-moved ('automatic'), i.e. spontaneous" (*Strong's Concordance*). It's the word we get our English word *automatic* from. When given the right conditions and time, the earth brings forth fruit automatically. There has to be this interaction between the seed (God's Word) and our hearts to get the desired harvest.

Scientists have discovered seeds thousands of years old that had never sprouted and produced fruit. But when the seeds were planted in the earth, they reproduced after their

A Sure Foundation

own kind. The miracle power that God put in the seeds wasn't diminished over time. They were as potent as the day they were produced, but they didn't germinate until planted in the soil.

And here is something that you may not have thought about: the seeds didn't produce the fruit. This verse says that *"the earth bringeth forth fruit of herself."* The seeds activated the potential that was in the earth, and the earth produced the fruit.

I imagine all of us have heard some statement like, "You can count the number of seeds in an apple, but you can't count the number of apples in a seed." Although there is a truth in that, it's not accurate that an apple seed produces an apple tree, which in turn produces more apples with seeds.

No! Mark 4:28 makes it clear that the ground is what brings forth fruit. The seed just activates the potential in the soil to produce the tree and then the fruit. If you don't believe that, then plant a seed in barren soil and see what you get. Nothing. The seed somehow draws out of the ground the potential that is already there.

An oak tree isn't in an acorn. Rather, the acorn has a miracle in it that activates the ground and draws out of the soil the nutrients that produce a huge oak tree. The oak tree is already in the earth, and the acorn just calls forth all the oak tree elements in the ground. If you plant an apple seed, it will call forth all the apple tree elements and so on.

This same thing is recorded in creation. Genesis 1:1 says, *"In the beginning, God created the heaven and the earth."* But when it came to the animals, God said, *"Let the earth bring forth the living creature"* (Gen. 1:24). And Genesis 2:19 says, *"And out of*

82

the ground the L<small>ORD</small> *God formed every beast of the field, and every fowl of the air."* This is very significant.

The Lord created the earth, but He formed the animals from what was already in the ground. This same thing happened with the body of Adam. Genesis 2:7 says, *"And the* L<small>ORD</small> *God formed man of the dust of the ground, and breathed into his nostrils the breath of life; and man became a living soul."* Everything that was needed to produce all the land animals and even Adam's body was already in the ground. The ground just needed a seed to activate it and bring those things forth. God's Word was the seed (Mark 4:14). Elephants, giraffes, dogs, cats, and every creeping and flying thing on the earth was at one time in the earth. God's Word just activated and brought out of the ground what God had already put in it.

I imagine that the Lord put huge amounts of thought and preparation into creation before He spoke things into existence. When He created the heavens and the earth, He put in the earth everything that He would need to form every animal He had imagined. They were already there as raw materials, but He had to bring them out of the ground by the miracle-working power of His Word, the seed.

Likewise, our hearts are the ground, and in our hearts is everything needed to produce whatever we need. The only thing missing is a seed. When the seed of God's Word is sown in our hearts, that seed immediately starts bringing forth the life that God put in the human heart.

We can see this in nature. If a fence post is left in the ground long enough, the ground will start eating it up. The ground will break down the elements in that post in an effort to bring forth fruit. The ground doesn't know the difference between an apple seed or an acorn or a fence post. It will take whatever is put in it and start trying to give it life. The earth just automatically tries to grow whatever is put in it.

This is good and bad. It's good when we are planting the seed of God's Word in our hearts, but it's bad when we let seeds of sin and unbelief be sown in. Our hearts just automatically start giving life to whatever we let dominate our attention. Sadly, most of us give much more time and focus to the negative things of this world than we do the eternal things of God's Word. Therefore, we need to root out the seeds of sin and unbelief and start planting the miraculous seeds of God's Word.

If understood and applied, this truth—that the seed of God's Word activates the miraculous potential of our born-again spirits—is amazing. We don't have to totally understand it (Mark 4:27). We just have to act on it, and our hearts will automatically produce the miraculous fruit that God intends from the seed sown.

Chapter 11

STEPS AND STAGES

Through this parable, we see that just like a harvest is dependent upon the sowing of seed, manifesting the kingdom of God in our lives is dependent upon the Word of God (Mark 4:26-29).

> *For the earth bringeth forth fruit of herself; first the blade, then the ear, after that the full corn in the ear.*

Mark 4:28

When you sow a corn seed, that seed doesn't just all of a sudden spring up and—*boom*—produce a huge stalk of corn with three ears on it. That's not the way it happens. Instead, the seed germinates, and there's a lot that happens under the ground before you ever see anything above the ground. But once growth starts poking up, it's first a little sprig, or a blade. Then the sprig continues growing up into an ear, and from there, it matures to a fully ripened fruit.

Although you might see an ear on a corn plant, you can't eat it if it's not mature yet. You have to let it continue to grow until it becomes a full, mature ear of corn.

For a tomato plant, first you get a small sprig, then a little blossom, and then a tiny tomato. But you have to let it grow until it fully ripens. A selling point that produce advertisers use for tomatoes is "vine ripened." In other words, it's better to let it ripen on the vine than to pick it green and then let it ripen. It has to be picked at the right time.

Work Your Way Up

This truth also applies to spiritual things. When you take the Word of God and start sowing it into your heart, you have to give it time to germinate. Then, even after you begin seeing some results from it and you know that the Word is producing, it never produces just instant victory. There are stages, or steps, toward victory.

There are always steps toward victory. You don't ever come from a position of failure and defeat into total absolute victory all at once. Now, that's what people desire. That's what they pray for all the time. But if you are going to take God's Word, sow it in your heart, and let it bring you to maturity and victory in your life, then there will be steps and stages along the way. That's what this parable teaches. That's what Mark 4:28

is saying. This is a law of God that never changes. There are necessary steps and stages to take as you move toward maturity and victory.

You can't go from zero to a thousand miles an hour instantly. There's an acceleration process. And if you tried to do it all at once, you'd be splattered up against the back windshield. You have to accelerate slowly and gain speed. It's the same way in the spiritual realm with your Christian life.

Maybe you are someone who comes from a background where you were told that God doesn't do miracles or heal people today. But now you have come into the revelation that God does heal, you're beginning to believe it, and you want to accelerate and see full manifestation of victory in this area of physical healing. You just want to see total healing and total deliverance, and you want to walk in perfect health right now. But do you know what? You would be ignoring this truth that first comes the blade, then the ear, and then the full corn in the ear. There are steps and stages.

If you don't start believing God on a small scale and work your way up, then you aren't going to experience complete victory. You don't go from being a person who has never applied God's Word in their life and never meditated on the Word, to all of a sudden being a person who has mountain-moving faith to overcome some incurable disease. It's not smart to wait until something hits—like a cancer that is beyond the medical profession's ability to help—before starting to believe God. It's unwise to expect to plant a seed and reap in the next week, trying to go from never having seen the Lord do a miracle in your life to seeing cancer healed miraculously, your tumor dissolving, all pain leaving, and everything being perfectly restored. There are steps and stages.

EXERCISE YOURSELF

What would happen if a farmer tried to do that? If he waited until he had an urgent need before planting his seed, but still expected to go out the very next morning to reap his crop and cash it in, he would go bankrupt. He wouldn't receive the money he needs from the crop. That's not the way it works.

If you want to see healing work in your life, you have to start where you are. Maybe it's just a cold or a headache. Many people think, *I'm not going to bother God with a headache.* But remember, the Word says it's first the blade, then the ear, then the full corn in the ear. There are steps. There are stages. There's growth involved. If you can't believe God to receive healing for a headache, then you can't believe God for healing from cancer.

Now, I'm not trying to discourage anyone who finds themselves in a situation where they have cancer but have never trusted God for deliverance from a headache in the past. You're in a situation where you don't have any alternative. You're going to have to jump in with both feet and start believing God. But if you don't have this track record, if you haven't grown and matured over a period of time, you probably need to go to someone else who has taken the Word of God and grown and matured. Let them pray for you and use their faith to help you to receive your healing.

If you're going to receive healing just through taking the Word and believing it, then there is a growth process involved. Preparation time is never wasted time. Even though you could take a pill to numb the pain of your headache and have relief in thirty minutes, practicing your faith is valuable. Or maybe you've been trying to believe God, but the headache has dragged on for a whole day now and you still have pain. You're thinking, *What's the use?* Well, what you don't realize is that until you start seeing this blade come up, until you start believing God for this small thing, you aren't going to be able to make this quantum leap into believing God for healing of cancer, or blind eyes opening, or deaf ears hearing. It is beneficial for you to sit there and fight that headache. Even though you could take a pill, you're exercising yourself unto godliness (1 Tim. 4:7-8).

NOT GOING TO HAPPEN

Years ago, one of our Bible college students came to me with a big idea. This man had some mental problems and had been in mental wards most of his life. Although he was thirty-something years old, he had never held down a job. His family had paid for him to be in these institutions. He lived off welfare and had never done anything financially on his own.

One day I was teaching on prosperity, believing God, and going out there and doing something—putting your hand to something that the Lord can bless. This man got excited and came to me to share his vision for restoring an old nearby hotel that had burned. The hotel was stone on the outside, so it was still repairable, but there was damage done on the inside. He had found it and was planning on buying it for about $2 million. Then he planned to spend over $3 million renovating it, after which he would be able to rent it out to people. He had figured out what the income would be per room so that he would pay for the cost of buying and renovating it. He had all this figured out and written down on paper, saying that God had spoken to him. He was going to believe God, buy this historic hotel, renovate it, and become a millionaire.

I went out of my way to compliment this fellow. Up until this point, he had been on welfare his whole life. He had never thought about doing anything. So, I commended him for dreaming and thinking big. But I also told him the truth. I said, "This is great, but it's not going to work for you."

He took offense at that, saying, "Are you coming against my faith, against what God told me to do?"

"Based on Scripture," I said, "there's always first the blade, then the ear, and then the full corn in the ear." I really loved this guy. I respected him and even liked him. But I told him, "You've never believed God for a dime. You've had your parents or welfare provide everything for you your entire life. You have never seen God give you a single dollar supernaturally, yet you're going to jump from never having had a dollar supplied to receiving $5 million? It's not going to happen. That's just not the way the kingdom works."

I told him to get a job and start earning his own living. Once he paid his own rent, bought his own food, drove his own car, and started paying his own way, I'd agree with him for bigger things. But going from zero to one hundred miles per hour instantly isn't acceleration; it's a wreck. It will kill you.

BEGIN SOMEWHERE

You have to begin somewhere. You have to start trusting God in the small things. Then, as you become faithful in a few things, God will increase you to more (Luke 16:10). This is a law of the kingdom. It's the way the Word works in your life. If you aren't trusting God with the little things—taking His Word and His promises that apply to your everyday life at work, at home, when your car stalls, or something else happens—how are you going to believe Him to overcome something big? Are you waiting until bankruptcy looms, until the doctor tells you you're going to die, or until the divorce papers are served before you start trusting God and applying His Word to your daily life? I'm telling you this in love, but if you do that, you're going to fail if you stand on your own. You'll have to go to somebody else and get help.

This is the way the kingdom works. If you want to believe God's promises and receive miracles, then you'll have to start applying His Word in small things. And it's going to be first the blade, then the ear, and then the full corn in the ear (Mark 4:28).

When we started ministering on television, I would have loved to be on every market in the entire world all at once. But even though I had been seeking the Lord and walking with Him for nearly forty years by this time, I wasn't to that stage. So, we only took on about $20,000 a month in television airtime. There were other costs too, like employees, equipment, etc., that probably added another $30,000 a month. That was a huge step for our ministry, but it wasn't the whole vision. I remembered this truth that there are steps and stages. Later we added another $50,000 a month in airtime, and we started covering a larger part of the globe. At the time of this writing, we're spending $1.3 million per month in television airtime. We're always taking steps of faith forward in the direction the Lord is leading, but not forgetting that there's always first the blade, then the ear, and then the full corn in the ear.

Growth in God's kingdom comes in steps and stages.

Chapter 12

DEEP FIRST

J esus said:

> *Whereunto shall we liken the kingdom of God?*
> *or with what comparison shall we compare it? It*
> *is like a grain of mustard seed, which, when it is*
> *sown in the earth, is less than all the seeds that be*
> *in the earth: but when it is sown, it groweth up,*
> *and becometh greater than all herbs, and shooteth*
> *out great branches; so that the fowls of the air may*
> *lodge under the shadow of it.*

Mark 4:30-32

Right after the Lord began showing me how important the Word of God was to my life, I started poring over it continuously. I mean, I meditated in it day and night (Josh. 1:8 and

Ps. 1:2). Then I got drafted into the US Army and went to Vietnam as a soldier. During my very first week in Vietnam, we had to complete some special CS gas training before they shipped us out to our final assignment. I remembered how in basic training I'd had a really negative experience with CS gas, which is basically the same thing as tear gas. CS gas burns your lungs, your eyes, your throat. It's just terrible.

I had an experience in basic training where they had us low-crawling under this wire. They said that when we heard the pop from the canister of CS gas opening, we were supposed to pull out our gas masks, put them on, clear them out, and get ready. It was a drill to see how fast we could do it.

Well, due to that bad first experience with CS gas, I hated it. So, this second time, I was ready. When I heard the pop and knew what it was—a canister of CS gas—I got my gas mask out and put it on. I was the very first person to secure my mask. A drill sergeant standing next to me kicked me and barked, "Trooper, what are you doing? I didn't tell you to put your mask on yet. Take it off!" So, I took my gas mask off. Then he stuck a canister of CS gas, which he had on the end of a stick, right in my face. I got a huge whiff of it, started choking, and tried to put on my mask. It was a terrible experience. He made me stand at attention, but I was choking and actually threw up in my mask. That made it even harder to breathe. I thought I was going to die.

A VOLUNTEER

So, when I arrived in Vietnam, we were scheduled to have this special training. They were going to put us through a gas chamber and then gas us with this CS gas to teach us how bad it was. Well, I was already absolutely totally convinced it was bad, and I did not want to go through any more of this. So, I remember praying and saying, "Lord, I'll do anything—*anything*—but You've got to get me out of this!" I was really believing God to deliver me from going through that gas chamber.

That morning at breakfast, they asked for a volunteer. One of the things you learn right away in the army is to never volunteer for anything. It's just not smart. However, at that point I didn't care what they were going to do. It didn't matter if they were going to use me for target practice—anything would have been better than this gas chamber. So, I volunteered. It turned out they made me the guard over the barracks that day. So, while everybody else went through the gas chamber, I just laid on my bunk in the barracks and studied the Word. It was awesome! I had a great time.

PUT DOWN ROOTS

I never will forget this. I was reading a passage of Scripture—Mark 4:30-32—about how the kingdom of God is like a little mustard seed. Have you seen a mustard seed before? I have. It's tiny. But once planted, it can grow into a very large plant. Jesus was saying that there is growth in the kingdom of God. We also read that in Mark 4:28, which says, *"First the blade, then the ear, after that the full corn in the ear."*

Through these scriptures, the Lord began ministering to me about how I needed to grow. This must have been around

January 1970, and I felt like that little mustard seed. I said, "God, I know You love me, and You've done something awesome in my life. But I am the smallest, most insignificant of all people. How in the world could You ever use me?" But this passage in the Word promised me that if I would take that seed—the Word—and plant it in my heart, it would produce this huge fruit. It would be like a tree that grows up so that the birds of the air can lodge under the shadow of it.

I remember lying on this bunk and just meditating and seeing myself someday growing to a place where I had something to help other people, where I would be able to bless other people. I remember thinking about this and, in my imagination, I saw this huge tree. It was like a giant oak tree spread out everywhere.

As I was thinking about this, pondering that picture in my imagination, the Lord spoke to me. He told me that if He granted me the growth that I wanted with the puny root that I had, the first bird that landed on one of my branches would topple the whole tree. I was so young in the Lord, with such little root, that the first puff of wind would blow me over. The Lord made it very clear to me that what I needed were roots and then growth would come later. The first thing to do was to put down roots.

BELOW THE SURFACE

Roots are below the surface. Even though they aren't normally seen, they stabilize and anchor the tree, drawing water, nutrients, and nourishment up into it. Roots enable all the rest of this above-ground growth to take place.

The Lord was showing me that my roots were not very deep. They were too shallow to handle the weight of what I was envisioning. If He had opened up a worldwide ministry and given me the opportunity at that time to share with people on that level, then the slightest little thing that came along would have toppled me over. Through this, the Lord really began to speak to me about some things.

You may desire some awesome things from the Lord. Perhaps you want great financial prosperity yet you haven't meditated on the Word of God and let that Word put roots deep down inside of you. First Timothy 6:9-10 says:

> *They that will be rich fall into temptation and a snare, and into many foolish and hurtful lusts, which drown men in destruction and perdition. For the love of money is the root of all evil: which while some coveted after, they have erred from the faith, and pierced themselves through with many sorrows.*

Now, there's nothing wrong with having prosperity. But what these verses are saying is that you need to have the root system and the stability to be able to handle prosperity in a godly manner. Without a deep root system in the Word, if God supplied, blessed, and gave you all that you desire, it would be the very thing that would ruin you. See, you need to let those roots go down deep first.

MORE CONCERNED ABOUT YOU

You may want to go out and work great miracles of healing and do all kinds of signs and wonders. But there are responsibilities, opposition, and temptations that go along with operating in such supernatural power, one of which is thinking that you did it yourself, instead of humbly admitting that it was God who used you.

There may be many things that you are looking for and praying for in your life that, if the Lord granted you right now, would absolutely destroy you. God isn't punishing you or doing bad things to you. Your heavenly Father only does good things for His children. But sometimes we perceive something as bad because it's not what we want in the moment. But He's trying to develop a root system on the inside of us.

God is more concerned about you than He is about using you to reach somebody else. He's more concerned about your integrity than He is about all of these other kinds of things. Through these parables in Mark 4, the Lord has taught me, "Don't worry about the growth above the ground. If you will take the Word and let it be rooted deeply on the inside of you, then this other growth will come." It's impossible to put a seed in the ground and let it develop roots without it also producing a tree or other plant above ground.

At the beginning of an oak tree's life, when the acorn first germinates, most of its energy is spent developing roots, with little growth above ground. Only with a dependable root system can that little acorn grow into a spectacular oak tree. And it takes time to develop roots like that.

HOLDING STEADY

Some people look at me and say, "My, how your ministry has grown. It just happened all of a sudden—overnight!"

Yeah, it's been a fifty-year overnight miracle. It may look as if the growth has happened all of a sudden, but what people don't know is that for fifty years I've been seeking God and establishing roots, holding steady and doing what He's told me to do.

There is a root system that needs to be developed in you, and that's what the Word of God does. It builds the character you need, and it keeps you from *being* a character. That's what we *all* need!

Chapter 13

COMMUNING
WITH HIM

As a kid, I grew up in Arlington, Texas. We had twenty-three pecan trees in our yard. My parents told me that it was my job to go around and pull up all the little pecan trees. Those pecans would fall down in the grass, leaves would cover them, and they would root themselves and begin to grow. Now, when they first came up above the grass, they weren't very tall. I could just go over and pull them up by hand. But being a typical kid, I wasn't really excited about pulling up these trees. So, I would let them grow until they were about a foot high. Then my parents would see them and would tell me I had to go pull up those pecan trees.

What I learned was that if I allowed one of those little trees to grow twelve inches above the ground, there would be all kinds of roots below the ground. If I let those trees get up to a foot high, then I'd have to get a shovel and dig them up to get rid of them. If I would have taken the opportunity when they were just a little bit above the ground, then I could have pulled them up by hand.

As I was meditating in my bunk that day in Vietnam, I wanted to be this huge tree with all kinds of fruit coming out of my life. I was thinking about all the above-ground things that were obvious to me and to other people. And the Lord spoke to me about my root system—which is below ground, where people couldn't see—being more important. He said, "If you have a good root system, the other will automatically come."

LIKE A TREE

You may be wanting God to use you and do things that are visible so that other people can see what the Lord is doing in your life. And yet you aren't spending time in your house alone with Him—reading, studying, and meditating on the Word—because that's not getting you a pat on the back. It's not visible. It's not something that you'll get any awards for.

But deepening your personal relationship with God, fellowshipping with Him, and learning about Him through the Word is what develops your root system. If you really want to be healthy and fruitful, that's what you have to do. You must develop your root system.

This is what Mark 4:30-32 is all about! Jesus said:

> *Whereunto shall we liken the kingdom of God? or with what comparison shall we compare it? It is like a grain of mustard seed, which, when it is sown in the earth, is less than all the seeds that be in the earth: But when it is sown, it groweth up, and becometh greater than all herbs, and shooteth out great branches; so that the fowls of the air may lodge under the shadow of it.*

Just like, in the natural realm, a seed needs to develop a root system before it can sustain any growth above ground, a believer must also spend time in the presence and Word of God. It's there that He'll work in their heart to develop a spiritual root system, something that will sustain them through hard times.

As a matter of fact, consider how a godly person is compared to a tree in Psalm 1:1-3:

> *Blessed is the man that walketh not in the counsel of the ungodly, nor standeth in the way of sinners, nor sitteth in the seat of the scornful. But his delight is in the law of the* LORD*; and in his law doth he meditate day and night. And he shall be like a tree planted by the rivers of water, that bringeth forth his fruit in his season; his leaf also shall not wither; and whatsoever he doeth shall prosper.*

A godly person is like a tree planted by a river of water. That's significant, especially in a desert climate! When a tree is planted by water, its roots can tap into that water source and bring continual nourishment, no matter what the weather is. That tree can be sustained and will stay strong enough to survive, even thrive, in the midst of severe weather and drought.

HARD TIMES

Everyone goes through seasons in life that are like a drought. Things happen to us that aren't necessarily from God or the devil. They're just natural things that happen.

When my wife and I were evacuated from our house due to nearby raging wildfires, one guy tried to tell me, "Well, if you were really believing God, this wouldn't have happened."

I don't look at it that way. We were in the midst of a drought, and the conditions were bad. It was so dry, a lightning strike or something like that could have set these fires off. It's not necessarily that God or the devil did it. Sometimes there are just natural things that happen. Now, I prayed to God and believed for supernatural results so that we'd still have a house, but if it had been burned, that wouldn't have made me feel like God was unfaithful to me.

It's no different than someone who builds a house on a beach and a hurricane hits it. I wouldn't think that God had failed them. If a person built a house that straddled the San Andreas Fault and then an earthquake came and damaged their house, it would be wrong for that person to get mad at God. There are some natural things that happen.

My wife and I live in the middle of a forest. So, when it's dry for a long time because of a season of drought, there's the potential of a forest fire. It's just like if a person lives on the beach, they have to deal with the potential of hurricanes. Or if someone lives on a fault line, they have to consider the possibility of earthquakes. It's not God or the devil that does it. It's just natural.

In life, you're going to go through things. Sometimes you may feel like you're going through a drought or a hurricane, or circumstances may shake you to your core like an earthquake. But when problems and situations come against you, the Lord can sustain you through it. Your root system—the relationship that you've built with God—will sustain you through hard times.

STABILITY

Do you have problems in your life? Are you cursing those problems and wishing they'd go away? Maybe you're thinking, *If I could just get God to solve this problem, get me a new spouse, a nicer house, a better car* ... Well, you're looking at all these things and thinking, *If I could just solve these problems, everything would be okay.* But do you know what your problem really is? It's your root system. It's the fact that you're shallow. You don't have any depth. You don't have the Word of God rooted deeply in your heart, and you can't dig down for that hidden nourishment. If you miss one single watering, you're going to wither, dry up, and die because you don't have any depth of maturity or true spiritual roots in you. Do you know what gives that to you? It's the Word of God.

"No, Andrew, I can be mature and grow spiritually and do all these things without spending a lot of time in the Word." Well, you can argue this point if you want to, but I know from experience that it's God's Word that has given me my relationship with Him. That's how He reveals Himself to me.

> *In the beginning was the Word, and the Word was with God, and the Word was God. . . . And the Word was made flesh, and dwelt among us.*

John 1:1 and 14

Jesus is equated with being the Word because He speaks through it. Jesus Christ is the Word of God made manifest (Rev. 19:11-16). When I study the Word of God, I'm studying Jesus. When I read the Word of God and God's Word speaks to me, Jesus is speaking to me. I am having a living, dynamic relationship with God through His Word.

To some people, that's just awkward. It's weird. They look at the Bible as just this book and say, "No, it's just a book. This is a book about God." No, it's not. When I am meditating in God's Word, I am communing with Him. He's speaking to me through this, which has produced my extensive spiritual root system and given me whatever stability I have in my life.

FIRST PLACE

You may say, "Well, I don't like this. I just don't think you have to do that." Really? Let's evaluate your life. Are you getting the fruit that you desire? Are things working in your life the way that you know God wants them to? If you're honest, in many areas of your life you'd have to answer, "No, they aren't." Well, then, if it's not working, maybe you ought to consider changing and taking advice from someone whose life is working. I'm not perfect, but my life is blessed. God is doing awesome things in and through me, and it's just like the Scriptures describe (Ps. 1:1-3 and Mark 4:30-32).

When I was lying on that bunk as a young soldier in Vietnam, the Lord spoke to me through these exact passages of Scripture. I wanted the fruit. I desired to be this huge tree that would provide shelter, shade, and nourishment to many people. And the Lord spoke to me, saying, "You don't have the root system to sustain this type of growth yet, but if you quit worrying about the growth and just let My Word take root deep inside you, that growth will come."

So, that's what I've done for the last fifty years, and there has been huge growth in my life, in my character, and in the number of people God has been able to touch through me. I'm telling you, this is what has worked for me. This was a *rhema* word from God to me, and it worked!

Do you want results like that? Do you want the power of God to begin to work in your life? Then you need to meditate on the Word of God and let it take root on the inside of you. I'm not talking about becoming casually acquainted with it, but coming to the place where you know God's Word better than the back of your own hand. You need to know God's Word better than you know what you look like.

God's Word has to become first place in your life. And if you will do that consistently over time, God's Word will put you first place in whatever endeavor He leads you to do. That's powerful!

Chapter 14

DON'T YOU CARE
ABOUT ME?

*And the same day, when the even was come, he
saith unto them, Let us pass over unto the other side.*

Mark 4:35

The same day as what? Well, the same day that Jesus taught
all of these parables about how the kingdom of God
grows in our lives like a seed. The Word of God is the seed, and
it must be planted in the soil of our hearts. But we can't pluck
it up and look at it all the time. We need to leave it in the soil
and let it take root. And there will be steps, stages, and seasons
to growth, maturity, and victory.

Every one of the ten different parables that Jesus taught that day emphasizes the importance of the Word of God and compares the kingdom of God to the natural world, where a seed has to be sown to produce a harvest. The Lord had been telling His disciples about how the Word works. He taught them about the kingdom. Jesus spoke to these disciples and then gave them a test.

At Charis Bible College, we have courses and classes. Once we're done teaching the lessons in a course, we give the students a test to see if they paid attention to, understood, and received what we were teaching. Basically, this is what Jesus did with His disciples.

A GREAT STORM

The Lord had been teaching them about the importance of the Word. He taught them how they needed to take the Word, act on it, and protect it. He taught them that the Word would do anything they needed. The Word is like a seed. If we use it properly, it'll produce a miracle and manifest God's kingdom (Mark 4:26-32).

After teaching them all this, the Lord put His disciples in a boat and tested them to see whether or not they would draw on what He had just taught them.

> *And when they had sent away the multitude, they took him even as he was in the ship. And there were also with him other little ships. And there arose a*

*great storm of wind, and the waves beat into the
ship, so that it was now full. And he was in the
hinder part of the ship, asleep on a pillow: and they
awake him, and say unto him, Master, carest thou
not that we perish?*

Mark 4:36-38

A great storm arose, they were about to perish, and Jesus
was asleep on a pillow in the back part of the boat. Can you
picture this?

I've been to the Sea of Galilee, and I've ridden in a replica
of the kind of ship they were on. It would have been an open
boat with no cabins below deck. The Word here says that their
boat was full of water (Mark 4:37). It looked like they were
going to drown, and Jesus was asleep on a pillow (Mark 4:38).
He wasn't in a lower cabin, so He must have been lying there
in the water.

PUT OUT

Either Jesus was sleeping supernaturally and was oblivious
to the fact that He was sloshing around in water in this huge
storm, or—which is more probable—He was aware of the situation but was just trying to sleep. A person couldn't be lying in
water like that and not be aware of the circumstances. I believe
Jesus knew what was going on but was still trying to sleep.

Here were His disciples, bailing water for all they were
worth and doing everything they could just to try to keep the

boat afloat. They looked over at Jesus, asleep, and woke Him up, crying, "Master, don't You care that we perish?"

These disciples were put out with Jesus. They were basically saying, "Lord, You aren't doing Your fair share. Here we are, about to drown, and You're sleeping. You do know that we're in a storm, don't You? You're sloshing around in the water just like we are, so how could You *not* know? Jesus, You just don't care. You don't care about us!" Now, there's no indication that they desired Him to perform a miracle. But they at least wanted Him to grab a bucket and help bail or take an oar and row. They just wanted Him to do *something*.

Lest we get too hard on the disciples, we often do the same thing. While talking with many, many people in different kinds of crisis situations, they've told me about their problem and how they were looking to God to bring them out of it. But because nothing had happened, they basically concluded, "God doesn't care about me. He doesn't care about what happened to me." It's the same type of attitude.

When you read the Word, you need to make correlations and applications to your personal life. Truth be told, almost every one of us has been guilty of doing the exact same thing that the disciples did. In the midst of a crisis, because we've felt like the Lord wasn't doing enough, we've said, "God, You don't care about me!"

WHY?

But look what happened when they woke Jesus up:

And he arose, and rebuked the wind, and said unto the sea, Peace, be still. And the wind ceased, and there was a great calm.

Mark 4:39

This was a miracle. There was this huge storm of wind, and the boat was full of water. Yet Jesus stood up, spoke three words, and instantly there was this great calm. That's awesome!

Although that was a great miracle, look what Jesus went on to say:

Why are ye so fearful? how is it that ye have no faith?

Mark 4:40

Notice the Lord's reaction. He didn't say, "Guys, I'm sorry. I was trying to get some sleep, but I should have been up. I should have been helping you. Forgive Me. I'm wrong, and you're right." That wasn't the Lord's response. Yes, He arose and took care of the problem, but then He turned around to the disciples and asked, "Why are you so fearful?"

Most of us would answer, "Why am I so *fearful?* The ship's going down! I'm about to die. What's wrong with You?"

But when the Word of God gets planted in your heart, it changes your view of things. You have a different way of looking at situations, and you aren't stressed out.

I Don't Need That

Years ago I came out of a neighborhood meeting concerning a wildfire in our area and the evacuation orders that were being issued at the time. It was certainly a crisis. The government was passing out these leaflets to the four or five hundred of us who were walking out after the meeting had concluded. One of the government employees asked, "Hey, do you want one?" I answered, "Sure, I'll take anything you've got." Then I stopped and read the title: "Stress Management—How to Recognize Stress & How to Deal with It." I just put it on the desk and said, "Thanks anyway, but I don't need that."

Some people might have thought, *You don't need that? You're in a crisis. You're being evacuated from your house. Why wouldn't you need that?* Because of the Word of God, I wasn't stressed out, worried, or bothered. Jamie and I are blessed. We had some people call us and ask, "Are you all right? Is everything going okay?" They were stressed out, and I was like, "We're fine, but what's wrong with you?" The difference in reactions was due to the influence of the Word of God.

Jesus didn't get up and say, "Guys, I'm sorry. I was insensitive. I wasn't aware of you." See, that's the attitude we are being pummeled with in our society. We are so touchy-feely that we're supposed to always empathize and feel other people's pain. But sympathy is all the world has to offer. We're taught to stroke one another and say, "Oh, I know it's bad." But Jesus has something better than that.

THE SAME TODAY

Jesus had been teaching the people, including His disciples, all that day about what the Word of God would do and how it would change them if they would put it in their hearts. When Jesus finally got up and took care of this situation, He didn't apologize and say, "You're right to feel this way." Instead, He rebuked His disciples, asking them, "Why is it that you don't have any faith? What's wrong with you guys?" Most of us would consider that unreasonable.

It's the same today. If someone comes into a crisis situation, most people say, "How dare you tell them that they can believe God and that they can do something? You need to just get down there and hug them, feel their pain, and empathize with them." I'm telling you that there is something better than just getting down in the mud and wallowing together in the muck and mire. We need to reach out a hand and help pull them up out of that stuff. The Word of God will change a person's heart so that they don't have to be overcome with things.

Jesus was like that. He asked, "What's the problem? Why don't you guys have any faith?" If they had taken the Word that was spoken to them—*"Let us pass over unto the other side"* (Mark 4:35)—and drawn the faith out of it that was available to them, they wouldn't have been so upset over the crisis situation. They could have taken care of it.

We need to start taking God's Word. Stop crying, "Lord, don't You care about me? Why haven't You done anything?" Instead we need to say, "Lord, I know why I'm not healed. I haven't meditated in the Word. The Bible says that Your Word is health to all my flesh and life to those who find it (Prov. 4:20-22). I'm going to get in there, start digging for myself, and find it!"

> *He sent his word, and healed them, and delivered them from their destructions.*
>
> **Psalm 107:20**

If you aren't taking the Word of God and meditating on it day and night, and if you aren't healed, don't get mad at God as if He's failed. He gave you healing right in His Word. But you aren't taking your "gos-pill" (Gospel). That's what the Word of God is; it's your "gos-pill." And you need to take it every day until you see the promised results.

Do you have a need? Then plant a seed—the seed of God's Word!

Chapter 15

POTENTIAL

J esus said:

> *Hearken; Behold, there went out a sower to sow: And it came to pass, as he sowed, some fell by the way side, and the fowls of the air came and devoured it up. And some fell on stony ground, where it had not much earth; and immediately it sprang up, because it had no depth of earth: But when the sun was up, it was scorched; and because it had no root, it withered away. And some fell among thorns, and the thorns grew up, and choked it, and it yielded no fruit. And other fell on good ground, and did yield fruit that sprang up and increased; and brought forth, some thirty, and some sixty, and some an hundred.*

> **Mark 4:3-8**

He continued, saying:

> *He that hath ears to hear, let him hear. And when he was alone, they that were about him with the twelve asked of him the parable. And he said unto them, Unto you it is given to know the mystery of the kingdom of God: but unto them that are without, all these things are done in parables: That seeing they may see, and not perceive; and hearing they may hear, and not understand; lest at any time they should be converted, and their sins should be forgiven them.*

Mark 4:9-12

The Lord was saying, "I have given you a special understanding so you can understand these parables. But people who aren't born again can't understand." I believe that the Lord did it this way to preserve these truths that cause the kingdom of God to operate. This prevents ungodly people from taking and using them to their advantage. It safeguards these truths for God's children.

FOUNDATIONAL

Jesus didn't use parables to hide truths *from* God's children, but *for* God's children. They are to give us an edge and knowledge of how His kingdom operates. All of this wisdom about how God intended this world to function has to be funneled through the Holy Spirit. Unless He makes these truths alive and helps us understand, we can't comprehend the things of God (John 6:63). That's what the Lord was telling His disciples.

> *And he said unto them, Know ye not this parable?*
> *and how then will ye know all parables?*
>
> **Mark 4:13**

Jesus revealed that this parable of the sower sowing the seed is so basic and so foundational that if we don't understand it, we won't be able to understand any of His parables. In other words, this parable is the foundation for all the teaching of Jesus. If we don't let the Holy Spirit unlock and make alive the truths contained in this parable, then we won't be able to understand any of Christ's teachings. Now that's a major statement!

This is like the key that unlocks all the rest of Jesus's parables, which means that we must get this parable. It's that basic. It's that foundational. So, let's go into the interpretation.

> *The sower soweth the word.*
>
> **Mark 4:14**

The Lord is not teaching us how to be farmers. He's using this illustration of how a seed works in the natural realm to tell us how the Word of God works in the spiritual realm.

HICK FROM TEXAS!

In Jesus's day, when a sower went out and sowed seed, they didn't have a tractor. They didn't use an implement of some kind to sow the seed in rows and space it like we do today. According to the way people sowed in that time, they dipped their hands into bags full of seed and then threw handfuls of seed out. They just walked along throwing seed everywhere. The seed fell not only onto prepared ground, but also on rocks and on places where there were already thorns and other things growing up.

Likewise, God has taken His Word and made it available to everybody. He has given His Word to us and granted us access to His Word. God has thrown His Word upon every type of ground, or heart, there is. Although there were four different kinds of ground discussed, only one out of the four brought forth fruit.

Every person who reads this book has access to God's Word. Right now, you are reading some truths from the Word that could change your life. You have access to those truths, but according to this parable, only a small percentage of the people who have access to the Word of God will ever really have it change their lives to the point that they bear fruit. It's not because God didn't sow the seed, but due to the condition of people's hearts.

Only one out of the four different types of ground really brought forth fruit and produced what the seed was capable of producing.

When the Lord first showed me these truths from this parable of the sower sowing the seed, I was just an eighteen-year-old boy. I had just gotten turned on to the Lord. I was excited because I knew that God had called me to minister and given me a vision to reach millions and millions of people with the truth of His Word. But I wondered, *How could I ever get that accomplished? I'm a hick from Texas!* If I were God, I wouldn't have picked me.

THE SEED

There's this guy on my television crew who has a golden radio voice. Yet I'm on this side of the camera, and he's on the other. I wouldn't have picked my voice to share the Word on radio and television. What was God thinking?

As a young man, I pondered this call and this vision, wondering, *Why did God call me?* But as I meditated on this scripture, the Lord spoke to me through this parable and gave me some truths that just changed my life. He showed me that it was the seed that caused the ground to bring forth fruit. The seed has the miraculous power of God in it to make the ground produce.

I was looking at myself and thinking, *Oh God, I'm not polished. I'm not a good speaker. I'm not well educated.* There I was, a total introvert who couldn't even look at another person in the face. I was focused on all of my weaknesses, shortcomings, and failures. But one of the truths that this parable taught me was that it's the seed that brings forth the fruit. The seed!

It wasn't the ground that had more that produced the best. Actually, it was the ground that had less that produced the best, because it had less rocks and less thorns. God began to show me that I could make myself good ground by just rooting out these things that I had allowed to take root in my life, things that hindered His seed. I started to see that I was just as capable of producing fruit as anybody else is, because it's not me—it's the Word. It's the Word that changes people's lives, not me. That was a real revelation to me!

This truth rang my bell! It gave me hope. I prayed, "Lord, if it's Your Word that produces the fruit, then I can study Your Word, learn Your Word, and speak Your Word the same as anyone else. If it's not based on my fancy clothes, polished voice, or attention-getting mannerisms, but it's Your Word that is going to change people, well then, praise God! Your Word can live in me the same as it can live in anybody." That gave me hope. That's powerful!

This really encouraged me. It's the seed, or God's Word, that has the potential. However, before the seed can release its potential, it first has to be sown into a heart.

PUT YOU OVER

As mentioned in a previous chapter, scientists have discovered seeds thousands of years old. When they took the seeds and planted them in the ground, the seeds began to germinate and produce plants. How awesome is that! Each tiny seed had this potential in it for thousands of years, yet it never released any of its potential until it was planted in the ground.

That's the way God's Word is. The Word of God is powerful. It's awesome what the Word can accomplish. But it's never going to release its power until it gets on the inside of you. Having a Bible sit on your coffee table isn't going to stop the devil. Carrying one under your arm won't either. You can lay a Bible on your head until it makes you flat on top, but it won't cause the blessings of God to come your way. You must take God's Word and devour it. The Word has to literally become a part of you.

These truths changed my life. They really did. It's God's Word that puts you over. It's God's Word that opens up doors. When the Lord showed this truth to me, I literally took it to heart. I've believed this parable with my whole heart ever since, and I realize that it's God's Word that changes people's lives—not me.

Maybe you're trying to hone your skills. You're going to school to learn marketing and business. You're studying courses on how to present yourself. You're learning all of these techniques and spending money on polishing yourself. You have the best-looking suits. You have your hair done. You do all kinds of things that, in their place, may be fine and helpful. But do you understand that it's the Word of God, the truth, and the revelation of God's Word that will really release the potential in your life? And this isn't only true of a preacher. This is true of anybody.

Many of my friends are immersed in the business world. Yet it's the truths of God's Word that have literally set them free and enabled them to prosper. This is for anybody. The Word of God will help a woman be a better housewife and mother. Honestly, I don't know how anyone can even conceive of being a parent apart from the revelation and truth that comes from God's Word. I mean, it's scary! It's tough enough being a parent *with* the Word of God. But without the Word it would be terrible! Raising kids is harder than raising the dead. I've had to do both, and it takes a miracle to see kids raised. You need the revelation of God's Word!

No matter who you are or what you do, the Word of God will put you over in every area of your life.

Chapter 16

STAY ON TRACK!

In the parable of the sower sowing the seed, there are four types of people, or soil, who received the Word of God. Concerning the first person, the Word says:

> *And these are they by the way side, where the word is sown; but when they have heard, Satan cometh immediately, and taketh away the word that was sown in their hearts.*
>
> **Mark 4:15**

The same parable recorded in the Gospel of Matthew phrases it a little bit differently.

> *Hear ye therefore the parable of the sower. When any one heareth the word of the kingdom, and*

> understandeth it not, then cometh the wicked one,
> and catcheth away that which was sown in his
> heart. This is he which received seed by the way side.

Matthew 13:18-19

This seed wasn't able to penetrate and get down on the inside. It's talking about a person who heard the Word but didn't *hear* the Word. It never got planted down on the inside of them. Did you notice the key? The key is understanding. The only type of person Satan had direct, unlimited access to steal the Word from was the one who didn't understand it. Understanding God's Word is vital. It's very, very important.

COMPLETE ACCESS

Understanding is the first step in getting the Word of God down in your heart. You must read the Word, pray, and meditate in it until you understand what it's saying.

This is precisely the reason we have children's church and youth ministry. The truths I teach in my meetings have the potential to set people free. I see blind eyes open and deaf ears healed. People are set free emotionally and spiritually from all kinds of bondages and addictions. I know that the Word I'm speaking works and changes lives. But when we have a conference or a convention, we also try to have youth and children's ministry whenever we can. This way, the young people can hear the Word presented in a manner that they can comprehend. If they don't understand it, then Satan is able to steal it away.

You need to present the Word in a way that people can understand. That's one reason I go out of my way to make the Word of God so simple. Some people have talked about me being so simple, sometimes I wonder whether it's a compliment or not. But as a whole, I believe that making the Word of God understandable is a very good thing. The smarter a person is, the more they ought to be able to make God's Word simple, easy to comprehend, and not complicated. Jesus was simple. That's why He taught with parables, or word pictures that communicate truths people can understand.

The very first type of person heard the Word but didn't have any understanding. If you can't understand what the Word is saying, Satan has complete access to steal those truths from you. And that's a terrible situation!

GET UNDERSTANDING

Wisdom is the principal thing; therefore get wisdom: and with all thy getting get understanding.

Proverbs 4:7

Not only do you need to have truths imparted to you, but you need to be able to understand and apply them too. Understanding is the ability to separate mentally. It's the ability to take truths and categorize them and put things together and say, "Oh, that's how this works."

If you're a mechanic, you know what a piston and a crankshaft are. If you're not, then you might have heard these words before, but you probably don't know how a piston and crankshaft fit together to make the motor work. You could have knowledge and yet be absolutely inept and unable to deal with a problem because you don't have the understanding to put things together.

It's the same thing with the Word of God. Many people know scriptures and can quote them, but they have no understanding about how a verse applies to their daily lives or how it links other truths of God's Word together. To get the Word of God down on the inside of a person and have it release its power, there has to be understanding.

And understanding is something that comes from God. It's something you can pray for. It's something you can seek. It's something that will come as a result of petitioning God and desiring it. In other words, you can make your heart receptive to understanding, or you can choose to harden your heart.

A HARDENED HEART

As a matter of fact, Jesus revealed that lack of understanding is one of the signs of a hardened heart.

> *And when Jesus knew it, he saith unto them, Why reason ye, because ye have no bread? perceive ye*

*not yet, neither understand? have ye your heart yet
hardened?*

Mark 8:17

A hardened heart will keep you from understanding, and
understanding will keep your heart from being hardened. You
need to let God soften your heart so you can begin to understand the truths of His Word. The first type of soil is the person who doesn't understand what the Word is saying, and the
devil is able to steal the Word away from them.

Mark 4:16-17 describes the second type of person, or soil,
this way:

> *And these are they likewise which are sown on
> stony ground; who, when they have heard the word,
> immediately receive it with gladness; And have no
> root in themselves, and so endure but for a time:
> afterward, when affliction or persecution ariseth for
> the word's sake, immediately they are offended.*

Affliction and persecution come for the sake of the Word.
This important piece of information has really blessed and
helped me through the years.

IT'S JUST BEGUN

Did you know that Satan isn't fighting you because of anything he has against you personally? You may feel that way

sometimes. You might say, "Man, the devil just has it in for me!" But that's not true. Satan is too busy trying to put out his own fires to deal with you on a personal level. What he comes against is the Word of God.

That means when you start getting a revelation of the Word, the battle isn't over; it's just begun. Now, that may put you off. You may be thinking, *Well, if that's the way it is, I don't think I want to start planting God's Word in my heart. I mean, the devil's going to fight me for the Word's sake.* Yes, I'm saying he'll fight you. But you'll win. You will be more victorious than you've ever been. But it won't be without a fight.

Lots of things have come against me. It would take me a long time to tell you about the things that have happened in my life and the things I've had to deal with. Sometimes it's nearly supernatural the way opposition comes against me. It seems like things happen to me that most people don't have happen to them. At one time I could have taken this very personally and thought, *God, why are You letting the devil be on my case like this?* But I've come to realize in a very real sense that it's a compliment. Satan is coming against the Word of God that is working in my life. He's trying to discourage me. And when I see that, instead of becoming discouraged, I just get more determined than ever. I realize that I have something valuable.

You need to recognize that afflictions and persecutions come for the Word's sake. They are coming against the Word of God to steal it out of your heart (Mark 4:17). Now, if you are very smart at all, that right there ought to tell you that God is not the author of the afflictions and persecutions. Why? Because He's not trying to get you to doubt His Word. Neither is He trying to steal His Word from you. Afflictions and persecutions come from the devil to stop God's Word in your life.

Sickness can get you so occupied in dealing with yourself that you quit taking the Word of God and sharing it with your friends. Afflictions can cause you to become so introverted and focused on your own problems that you forget other people. These things can steal the Word from you. Persecution might cause you to think, *If this is the way I'm going to be treated every time I take a stand for God and say what's right, I'm not sure I want to do that.* Affliction and persecution are designed to cause you to stop ministering the Word, to stop living the Word, and to stop drawing on the results that the Word promises. That shows you who the author is. Satan is the one who is bringing problems into your life, not God!

YOU HOLY ROLLER!

The purpose of persecution is to stop God's Word from continuing to work in your life. So, even if you still believe the right thing but are timid and shy in your convictions, then the devil has accomplished his purpose. You might still hold to the same doctrine. But if you quit speaking and sharing the Word with other people because of the persecution that it's going to draw, then Satan has achieved his goal.

If you're at work and somebody is sick, and you stand up and say, "I believe that God heals," but then everybody turns on you and says, "You holy roller!"—that's persecution. And if that causes you to quit speaking the Word of God, then Satan won. Whether you ever change your belief that God is the Healer or not, if you back off your stance and quit sharing truth with others because you're afraid of persecution, then the devil's plan worked. The purpose of persecution is to stop the Word. If it stops you from speaking and acting on God's Word, then persecution has won.

I was in a very dead church when I first got really turned on to the Lord. So, when I came alive in God and started operating in the Word, I experienced a lot of opposition and criticism. Everybody was telling me how wrong I was, and that didn't feel good. It offended me. I was hurt. These people were friends of mine before this. But now, because I was excited about God and His Word, they had turned on me. I'm talking about church people and not secular friends. I was criticized in the church!

During this time, I went to a Joe Nay meeting. He's the guy who got me started in the ministry. I went to his meeting frustrated and hurting because of what people had said about me. I had been defending myself and arguing with them, yet I wasn't winning the arguments. Joe called me out and gave me a prophecy. He said, "I see you like a runner on a track. You're running and leading the pack. You're doing great, but people in the grandstands are yelling at you. They're saying that you're doing it all wrong. I see you getting off the track and going up into the grandstands, arguing with the crowd. Even if you win the argument, you're going to lose the race. Forget what the people are saying and stay on track. Stay on track!"

STAND FOR THE WORD

Friend, you too need to stay on track. God didn't call you to be up in the grandstands. Someone yelling at you and criticizing you cannot stop you from winning unless you get off the track. And that's what persecution is designed to do; it's designed to get you off track. It's to get you licking your wounds and trying to justify yourself. It's to get you thinking, *God, look what they said about me.* What people say about you isn't important. It's the message that's important. It's what He's given you to say. It's the Word of God!

You need to recognize what's happening. When your coworkers criticize or make fun of you at work, you need to realize that they didn't do that until you took a stand for the Word of God. It's not you who is being persecuted. They're coming against the Word. Satan is inspiring and using these people (Eph. 6:10-13). The purpose is to get you to shut up and quit acting on and speaking the Word of God. That's what's going on.

The Lord shows us this truth through the parable of the sower sowing the seed. This is one of the ways the devil steals the Word from you. If you ever get to where you are hurt and licking your wounds, trying to justify yourself, and backing off the Word of God, then—according to this parable—you aren't going to bear fruit. The Word will cease to produce and release its life in you. That's not what you want. You want better results than that. And if you recognize that this is one of the ways that Satan tries to steal the Word from you, it'll make a big, big difference in your life.

Chapter 17

STICK WITH
THE WORD

In the parable of the sower sowing the seed, stony ground represents the second type of person who heard the Word. There was some dirt there, some earth that the seed could germinate and take root in, but the end result was that this person didn't bring forth fruit either. Satan was able to stop it.

> *And these are they likewise which are sown on stony ground; who, when they have heard the word, immediately receive it with gladness; And have no root in themselves, and so endure but for a time: afterward, when affliction or persecution ariseth for the word's sake, immediately they are offended.*
>
> **Mark 4:16-17**

This type of person becomes excited about the Word of God, but they don't take time for the Word to get rooted on the inside. Because they don't have any root in themselves, the Word doesn't work.

Sad to say, I believe that most people who claim to be excited about the Word are in this realm. Truthfully speaking, the Word is just surface level with them. They haven't really committed their lives to it. God's Word is not something that is foundational in their lives. They're excited about the Word until it begins to cost them something.

I was born again at eight years old. Then, at age eighteen, I had a miraculous encounter with the Lord where I knew that He loved me. Shortly after that, God began to show me the importance of His Word. As I went through Vietnam as a US Army soldier, I began to establish a foundation that was built on the Word. I had been in a Baptist church before I went to Vietnam. After I returned from serving my country, I still attended a Baptist church, but my theology had grown beyond that. I was teaching truths I saw in the Word, truths like it's God's will to prosper you, it's God's will to heal you, God loves you, God isn't putting problems in your life, God's not punishing you, etc. This wasn't accepted by the Baptists, so I was beginning to get some flak over it.

It was strange at first. I didn't realize what was happening. Before I went into the army, and as long as my theology was consistent with theirs, these people loved me. They threw me a going-away party and everything. But after fourteen months of being in the Word day and night, my theology had changed somewhat. I was believing for miraculous things. And when I came back, I began to share that. These people who had been my friends and had sent me away with a party were now beginning to reject me. I was getting criticism galore. At first, I didn't realize what was happening, and it caused me to shrink back a bit.

THE PATTERN

During this period of time, I was living in Arlington, Texas, and attending a Baptist church about forty miles away. In the other direction was Kenneth Copeland in Fort Worth, Texas. Now, this would have been about 1972, and Kenneth was just getting started. He was just beginning to be popular, but let me tell you, he rang my bell! Kenneth just blessed me. So, I would go over to his meetings and get so fired up. Then I would come back to this Baptist church and teach the truths I had heard to my Sunday school class.

For a week or two, miracles would manifest. We would see people healed. There would be great results and wonderful things happening, but then the leadership of the church would find out about it. They'd come in and criticize me, saying, "You aren't teaching from the quarterly. You're teaching false doctrine." They came against me big time. I never did say, "All right, I'm wrong; I reject these things." I still believed the Word, but I did become offended.

And have no root in themselves, and so endure but for a time: afterward, when affliction or persecution

> *ariseth for the word's sake, immediately they are offended.*
>
> **Mark 4:17**

That was happening to me. I wasn't rejecting what I knew to be true, but I was losing my enthusiasm, my boldness, and my confidence about it. So, after about two weeks of criticism, I'd get back to where I was preaching those same truths, but we weren't seeing any miracles. We weren't getting any results. It was different. It didn't have the life and anointing of God on it. I couldn't figure it out!

Then I'd attend another Kenneth Copeland meeting in Fort Worth for two or three days. I'd get so pumped and fired up that I'd come back and preach those truths in the Baptist church, and the same thing would happen. Miracles would manifest, and people would be set free. Then I'd get criticized and become offended. So, I'd back off those truths in my heart, saying the same things but getting different results. And that would go on for a month or two. Then Kenneth Copeland would hold another meeting, and after a while, my lightning-fast mind began to notice a pattern.

GOD TOLD ME

I wondered, *What's happening?* The Lord used this exact passage of Scripture to say, "The problem is that you're excited about the Word, but you don't have any root in yourself. It's not your revelation. It's not what I am speaking to you. You are parroting what Kenneth Copeland is getting from Me. That's the reason the Word isn't producing. You just don't have root. It's not you."

I am very grateful for the influence Kenneth has had on my life and ministry. He was very instrumental in getting me started. However, once God spoke to me through Mark 4:17, I made a decision right then. I said, "From now on, I'm not going to say, 'Kenneth Copeland said,' 'Kenneth Hagin said,' or 'Billy Graham said.' It's going to be, 'God told me.' It's going to be personal revelation." I made a decision, and when I did that, my life began to change drastically.

That's the reason I seldom refer to anybody else. It's not because other people haven't had an influence in my life. It's just that if I hear something from them, I take it and meditate the Word on it until it's no longer what somebody else said. It's "This is what God told me."

That's the way the Word of God has to be in your life for it to produce.

ANYBODY

A certain woman was very influential in my life in our early days of ministry. She was like my spiritual mother. Jamie was like her best friend. We spent a lot of time together. This woman really spoke into my life. Well, as I started getting stronger and stronger in the Word, what I believed began to differ more and more with what she believed. This woman would drop little hints here and there. It would be hard to call it persecution because she wasn't being malicious. She wasn't trying to do us damage. She really loved us and thought she was doing good. Nonetheless, her little pecking away and constant criticism of everything I said was persecution. It was an affliction. It was trying to get me to back off the Word. Jamie and I had seen this, but we had never taken a stand against it because we respected her. She was like a spiritual parent.

Then one Saturday night, Jamie and I were studying the Word. The Lord showed me these exact verses of Scripture (Mark 4:16-17). Through them He said, "The problem with you is that the Word isn't rooted in you. You're taking someone else's revelation. It's not a total revelation to you." When I saw that, Jamie and I joined hands, prayed, and declared, "From now on, we're going to make God's Word personal to us, and it won't matter who says what. If God has told us something and we know it, we aren't going to let anybody—*anybody*—steal that from us."

The very next morning, we went to church. That afternoon, this woman, who was like a spiritual mother, called Jamie into a back room to speak to her. She warned, "Jamie, you're the only one who can do anything about Andrew. He's gone so far with this that you're the only one who can stop him. You need to get him to renounce these things that he's saying God is showing him. This isn't God."

My wife and I had just made this decision the night before, so Jamie looked her right in the eye and responded, "You know what? That's my husband. I'm sticking with him. I believe that this is God speaking to us, and from now on, this relationship is over."

Now, that may not have been the best way of dealing with the situation. But at that time and place, and because of how immature we were, we weren't able to sit there and debate. That was really the only way we knew how to handle it. Jamie came and told me what happened. So, I talked to this woman and her husband, and basically, we left that church.

We cut off that relationship, and it was more than ten years before we had any communication with those people. But God put the relationship back together. It's a powerful story. We've become very close friends once again, and I minister to this woman a lot. We have a wonderful relationship now because God restored it. But for a period of time, we literally had to make a decision that nothing and no one was going to come between us and the Word. If they were going to come against the Word, then we were going to stick with the Word.

EXTREME MEASURES

You might be thinking, *Boy, Andrew, that's just a little too severe. That's more than I'm willing to do. I don't believe that's right.* Well, again, if I had been more mature at the time, I might have been able to deal with that situation differently, but I wasn't. I don't think I could have dealt with it any differently at the time.

It's like when a little plant is very young and small, it has to be put in an incubator or a hothouse. The environment has to be controlled because the plant is very susceptible to the elements. It can't withstand a snowstorm or go through a hurricane. It has to be put in a hothouse and protected.

Now, after the plant gets rooted and the roots are down deep, that's a different story. It was the same with me. Once the roots of the Word grew down deep in me, somebody could have said those things to me and I could have turned away and not had to totally separate myself from them. And this is all because of a deeper root system. I can now withstand things that I couldn't withstand then. Does that mean I was totally wrong in the way we did it? It's the only way I knew how to do it. I don't think I could have done it any better at that time.

I'm just saying that this is the degree of commitment that's necessary. Now, if you are more mature and are able to handle it differently, that's fine. But you must have this same level of commitment to the Word. You have to be willing to declare, "God's Word is going to be first place in my life, no matter who or what comes against me. I don't care if it's my best friend, the pastor, or the church I grew up in. I don't care if I've got my name engraved on a pew in the church or on one of the bricks outside. It doesn't matter. If something's going to be stealing God's Word from me, then I'm going to take a stand and do whatever it takes to protect the Word that's on the inside of me."

You might think I'm overemphasizing this and making more out of it than what it is, but I really do believe that there is a spiritual battle raging in every single person. The battle isn't over how attractive you are, how much charisma you've got, your skills, or your talents. Those things are really immaterial. The battle raging is over the Word, and Satan is trying to get you to back off from it. He's trying to get you to compromise or neglect God's Word. This is really what it's all about.

REALITY

Keep the Word of God foremost in your life and preeminent in your heart. Meditate in it day and night!

> *This book of the law shall not depart out of thy mouth; but thou shalt meditate therein day and night, that thou mayest observe to do according to all that is written therein: for then thou shalt make thy way prosperous, and then thou shalt have good success.*

> **Joshua 1:8**

If you meditate in the Word of God day and night, you will make your way prosperous and have good success. God's Word is what will cause success in your life.

It doesn't matter your station or vocation. You could be a minister, a housewife, a father, a mother, or a businessperson. It doesn't matter what you're doing, the Word of God is what will strengthen you in every area of your life. Your relationship with God, your relationships with other people, your family, your work, your prosperity, your health—the Word will strengthen anything! It's all dependent on what you do with God's Word.

And it can't just be you taking someone else's revelation and operating from that. You need to take that revelation and meditate the Word on it until it gets rooted on the inside of you and you put down roots. Then the Word of God will begin to produce.

This second type of person didn't take the time to let the Word of God become reality in their life. So, the devil was able to use affliction and persecution to hinder the Word in their heart. What about you?

Chapter 18

ROOT, THEN FRUIT

Notice what the Word says about this second type of person: the stony ground.

[They] *have no root in themselves.*

Mark 4:17, brackets added

In other words, they were receiving their nourishment from someone else, and they didn't have root in themselves.

Because the power of God lives on the inside of you, you don't have to always be going through another person to reach Him. If you are born again, God Himself lives on the inside of you. You can tap into His life, but it's just like a seed. A seed has to put roots down to be able to go down inside the earth and bring up minerals and water. This is why trees flourish when they are planted along a stream or beside an aquifer. They grow bigger and better than other trees because their roots are able to tap into the water.

The reason a plant in stony ground doesn't really bear fruit is that it isn't able to go down deep and tap into any type of nourishment.

SUSTAIN GROWTH

My sixth-grade teacher had two identical terrariums. He put soil in both of them. One of the terrariums had soil about an inch deep. The other had soil about a foot deep. My teacher put tomato seeds in both terrariums and watered each one the same every single day. He kept these terrariums at the front of the class, so we watched as the seeds began to release their miracle. The seed in only an inch of soil sprang up and produced a plant nearly a foot tall before the other seed even put a little sprout above the ground.

It looked like the seed in shallow soil was doing better, but the reason is that the roots couldn't grow down. There wasn't anywhere for them to go. The seed had enough soil to germinate, but not enough to sustain growth. Because the growth couldn't go into the roots, it all went above ground. After the plant got about a foot tall, it turned white, shriveled up, and died. It didn't have the root system to sustain itself.

The other plant, which was only a tiny sprout by that time, began to grow and flourish. It produced full tomatoes and was fruitful.

Through this example, I've learned a valuable lesson. We cannot expect to have growth above ground that is greater than the growth we have beneath the surface. In other words, the root system is the biggest area of growth.

Do you want fruit? Then grow your roots. Many people desire to see the power of God manifest in their lives and good things happen, but they don't let the Word of God take root in their hearts. They just want the fruit. They don't want to spend time in the presence of God, seeking Him and serving Him. They just want to see the power of God in manifestation. That isn't the way it works. Any more than a tree can sustain growth without a root, you cannot sustain fruit in your life without a good root system.

GODLY CHARACTER

This is the same truth that God spoke to me when I was on my bunk in the barracks in Vietnam that day He delivered me from the gas chamber drill. I was meditating on these scriptures, the parable of the mustard seed, and God gave me this vision of the huge tree with tiny roots (Mark 4:30-32). The bird landed on the tree, and the tree fell over because it didn't have much of a root system. Through this, the Lord started speaking to me. He said, "Andrew, you want this huge growth, but your root right now is very shallow. If I were to answer your prayer and give you the growth you're desiring right now, it would destroy you."

Do you want the Lord to use you? Are you desiring fruit? Do you want to see the Word of God work? Well, how much time have you put into letting the Word of God take root on the inside of you? It's actually the mercy of God that is keeping you from being used to a greater degree. And it's the mercy of God that has kept you from prospering more financially, because you don't have the character yet to be able to handle it. I know that's not necessarily exciting news, and you may not feel real blessed by this revelation, but it's true. This is the real answer.

God has established laws in His kingdom that make it so you can't grow beyond your root system. He did that because He loves you, not to damage, hurt, or hinder you. The Lord doesn't want you to grow above ground more than you've grown below the ground. Another way to say it is, you can't grow more outwardly than you've grown inwardly. If you haven't let the Word of God grow on the inside of you—shaping and molding you into a person of godly character—then that's going to stunt any manifestation of God's Word working in your life in these other areas.

Do you desire healing in your body, increased prosperity, and open doors for ministry? Do you want better relationships or promotion to a greater role of leadership and influence in your job or church? Do you desire for God to use you to make a bigger impact on other people's lives? These are all good things that the Lord wants for you, but they are fruit produced by the Word of God taking root more deeply on the inside of you. To see increase in fruit above the surface, you have to let God's Word take root below the surface.

Private Relationship

Letting the Word take root on the inside of you is similar to a seed's roots growing under the ground. This isn't done out in public or in front of people. This is in your own private relationship with God.

Maybe you've heard me share some testimonies of the fruit the Word of God is producing in my life and you're saying, "I wish I could have some of the miracles you've talked about. I want to see blind eyes open, deaf ears hear, and people raised from the dead. I desire to see people healed from all kinds of sicknesses and diseases. I'd sure like to walk in peace, provision, and blessing no matter what's happening around me. I just wish the Word of God would work for me that way!"

What you don't understand is that I have spent years meditating on the Word of God and letting it take root on the inside of me. You might see some fruit in an area of my life and think, *Well, that looks easy. I want that*, and you're going straight for the fruit. But what you need to do is go straight for the root.

I used to spend a lot of time asking God to use me. One day He said to me, "Stop asking Me to use you. The reason I'm not using you is because you aren't usable. Rather, pray, 'Lord, make me usable.' I want to use you more than you want to be used. The moment you get usable, I'll put you to work." That all has to do with your root system.

If you would just take care of letting God's Word produce roots in your heart, then eventually the Word will grow and bear the fruit you desire. It takes much root to bear much fruit!

Chapter 19

CHOKED

Mark 4 talks about four different types of ground, which are four different types of people who hear the Word. Another way of looking at it is that there are also four progressive stages your heart goes through in receiving the seed of God's Word.

The first stage is when the heart is so hard that God's Word doesn't even seem to penetrate it. That's the first type of person described.

Then you go through a time where the Word of God excites you, you're enthusiastic about its potential, but you aren't ready for the rejection and criticism that come your way for beginning to take a stand on the Word. If you don't overcome the afflictions and persecution and move through this stage, then the Word of God will never bring forth fruit. You have to get to a place where you say, "I'm going to stand on the Word of God even if it costs me relationships, if I get punished, fired from a job, or whatever. I don't care. God's Word is all-important!"

CARES, DECEITFULNESS, LUST

Then there's a third type of person, or a third stage your heart has to move through. It's described in Mark 4:18-19, which says:

> *And these are they which are sown among thorns; such as hear the word, and the cares of this world, and the deceitfulness of riches, and the lusts of other things entering in, choke the word, and it becometh unfruitful.*

This is powerful! I pray that the Lord is giving you revelation and you're seeing this progression.

I remember when God used Mark 4:16-17 to speak to me. Through these two verses, He showed me that I did not yet have roots in myself. I was living off someone else's revelation. Then I made a decision that the Word was going to become real to me. Once I made that decision, I began to move into Mark 4:18-19 (see above). Personally, I believe that, to some degree, I'm still in between the third type of soil and the fourth type of soil, where fruit really starts to produce. I'm seeing some fruit in my life, and I praise the Lord for what He's doing, but I know there's more.

The third type of soil (or heart) is where you've made the commitment to go on, regardless of what it might cost you.

You've decided that the Word of God is going to dominate your life. But notice again what Mark 4:19 says:

> *The cares of this world, and the deceitfulness of riches, and the lusts of other things entering in, choke the word.*

ADDICTIVE PERSONALITIES

When a person gets ready to plant a natural seed in the soil, they usually till the ground, remove all the grass and weeds, and then put their seed in there. They begin to water the seed and start looking for results. Even though they've pulled out the old grass and weeds, some hidden seeds will remain, and weeds will begin growing along with their new plant. What they have to do is carefully remove all of these weeds and leave their plant undisturbed. If the weeds aren't removed, they will sap the strength and nutrients that the plant needs. It seems like weeds (what you don't want) always grow bigger and faster than the fruit of God's Word (what you do want).

It's the same in the spiritual realm with the seed of God's Word and the soil of your heart. The Word of God begins to take root in your heart, but your heart will want to latch on to other things.

Take sports, for instance. (Now, if this is you, I'm not trying to criticize or pick on you. I'm simply making an application so you can understand what I'm talking about.) I've met people who treat sports like a god. They watch anything with the word *sports* in it and spend huge amounts of time sitting in front of the television.

Now, there's nothing wrong with sports, in moderation. Just about anything done in moderation is okay. That's what the Scripture teaches. But many people tend to be extremists. They have addictive personalities. So, they literally just plant themselves in front of the screen during the season of their favorite sport.

"PHS"

Many women have come to me saying, "My husband is in this stupor. He just can't do anything except talk about sports." One woman told me, "My husband has PHS."

I thought, *Oh man, what is this, some new disease?* So, I asked her, "What is PHS? What does it do to your husband?"

She answered, "He just sits on the deck in a chair and stares out into the woods. He'll sit there polishing his rifle and cleaning his gun."

"So, what is PHS?"

"It's Pre-Hunting Syndrome. About the time fall begins, he just gets this glazed look in his eyes. He becomes captivated by thinking about going out there and trapping, hunting, and doing things related to that. I just lose him for months!"

That's the kind of thing Mark 4:19 is talking about. We shouldn't be involved in something to such a degree that it takes us out of the Word of God.

DIVERT AND OCCUPY

The cares of this life also include things like parenting, working a job, or all kinds of other things that certainly aren't sinful. As a matter of fact, Second Thessalonians 3:10 says, *"If any would not work, neither should he eat."*

Work is good and has its place in our lives. But we can be so occupied with making a living and raising our children that it will literally choke the Word of God in our hearts and keep it from producing in our lives. We can successfully pass the threshold to where affliction and persecution aren't big things. But a much more subtle and deadly attack of the devil against the Word of God in our lives is simply preoccupation with other (not necessarily sinful) things.

If you want to destroy a person's vision, give them two. Divide their vision, and they'll end up with "die-vision" (division). We simply can't do multiple things wholeheartedly and correctly. We have to establish priorities. There must be certain things in our lives that are such a high priority that we never depart from them. Every day for the rest of our lives we are going to establish these priorities. If we want the Word of God to really produce in our lives, it has to become a priority. The subtlest way that Satan comes against us is through things that aren't necessarily sin, but they divert and occupy our time and attention.

SO BUSY

Like a parcel of ground, you only have so many nutrients in you. And if those nutrients are depleted, it won't matter if the best seed in the world is planted in your heart, the seed won't produce. If your heart is given over to other things and your time and attention are elsewhere, you can choke the Word of God.

> *The cares of this world, and the deceitfulness of riches, and the lusts of other things entering in, choke the word, and it becometh unfruitful.*

Mark 4:19

As a minister, I've been through several different stages in my life. There was a time when people stayed away from my meetings by the droves. I mean, it was just supernatural how many people didn't come. So, during that season I just spent a huge amount of time in the Word of God.

Then we started seeing miracles, and some folks had their lives changed. People started coming. When I moved to Pritchett, Colorado, there were times that—if I had allowed it—I wouldn't have been able to sleep at night. People were staying over until late, and I had to send them home. They'd wake me up at two, three, or four o'clock in the morning. Miracles were happening so fast, but I was being run ragged.

I went weeks with only ever opening the Bible to minister the Word through prayer and preaching to other people. It's not that ministering was bad. It's that I was so occupied with ministering to other people that I wasn't sowing the Word into my own heart. What was occupying me wasn't a bad thing. It wasn't anything evil. It was actually helping people. But we can get so busy helping people that it destroys our personal relationship with God.

QUALITY AND QUANTITY

What I'm trying to say is this: If the Word of God can be choked by being occupied with helping, praying for, preaching, and ministering to people, then how much more can a person be preoccupied by their job or a favorite sport or television show? We can become preoccupied to such a degree that the Word of God is not able to release its power and produce fruit in our lives. Part of being a fruitful Christian is taking the needed and regular time to sow God's Word into our hearts.

One time I hosted a major conference and was very busy. I was going nonstop from six in the morning until after midnight each day. I just didn't have very much time to study the Word. So, after the conference, I spent a couple of days just kicking back. Although I had a lot of things I needed to do, I went out of my way to just sit in the Word and study. I wasn't studying to minister the message or to have something to give to somebody else. I was reading and meditating on the Word for me, which is what I've been doing now for more than fifty years.

You might be thinking, *All right, how long do I have to be in the Word? Will six months do it, and then I can get this?* You're missing it. You have to get to where the Word of God is a lifestyle with you.

As a matter of fact, I've read Psalm 19 hundreds, if not thousands, of times. And that is no exaggeration. There's a song I sing based on that chapter, and I've sung it hundreds, if not thousands, of times. And yet I always get some new revelation out of it. But it's really not new; it's just a new way of seeing it. And I guarantee you, this revelation is going to bear fruit in my life. I'm getting brand-new insights from God's Word every single day.

For many people reading this book, that's not your lifestyle. You want the fruit, but you aren't going to plant the Word in your heart and protect it. You're going to let other things occupy your time. I'm telling you in love that that's not the way the Word of God works (Eph. 4:15). You have to spend quality time *and* quantity time in the Word of God.

QUIET TIME

My wife and I raised two boys. When they were little, they were energetic, bounced off the walls, and played. But we had a quiet time every afternoon. It didn't matter where we were or what we were doing, there was a quiet time. When they were really young, Jamie laid them down and made them take a nap. As they got older, they didn't always have to sleep, but they had to be still and do something quiet, like read a book or look at pictures. They had to have some quality downtime. We taught our kids how to kick back and rest every single day instead of just be constantly going.

Maybe you can't relate to that, but I don't believe that our children are exceptions. I think that most people have indulged their kids and spoiled them in that area.

During that period of time, my wife forced herself to take that hour off. In the natural, it would have been a great time to get some work done without two little boys in tow, but she determined to spend that time praying, studying the Word, and recharging her batteries because it takes a lot of energy to raise kids. There are ways that you can do this.

When I'm talking about being in the Word of God, I recognize that we can't always be sitting and reading. However, we can meditate in the Word day and night.

A GREATER SATURATION

This book of the law shall not depart out of thy mouth; but thou shalt meditate therein day and night, that thou mayest observe to do according to all that is written therein: for then thou shalt make thy way prosperous, and then thou shalt have good success.

Joshua 1:8

Now, you can't always be reading the Word and still have a full-time job, raise kids, etc. But there is a certain amount of time that you must spend sitting and reading, because you can't meditate on what you haven't put in you. Once it's in you, you can develop a lifestyle where you keep your mind stayed on the Word (Is. 26:3). For instance, you can listen to godly Christian music instead of secular music. Why listen to folks singing about people falling off a barstool, wailing, travailing, and all kinds of discouragement? Listen to something that glorifies God, whether you're driving in your car or working at home.

The advances we have in technology today give us many options for listening to the Word. There really is no reason that people today can't have a greater saturation of the Word of God than people had in previous decades. Our lifestyles may be busier, but we have some advantages. We can turn on Christian radio, Christian television, and Christian podcasts. We can listen to audio recordings of preaching, teaching, and even the Word being read aloud. We can meditate in the Word of God day and night (Josh. 1:8).

"Well, Andrew, I just don't like that. I like all this other stuff." Well, if you like that fruit better than you like the fruit of the Word of God, it's your choice. You don't have to do what I'm saying to be able to love the Lord and go to heaven. As a matter of fact, you can probably get there quicker because when you get sick, you won't be able to draw on the power of God. You'll have to wait on a healing evangelist to come through town. Or if your situation is a crisis, you'll die and go to heaven early because you won't know how to receive healing. Meditating on the Word isn't a necessity. It's not mandatory— unless you want fruit. If you want fruit, then you have to root out the other things that vie for your attention, and you need to put priority on meditating in the Word of God.

I don't know how to totally explain this, but when you meditate on God's Word, it just changes you. It changes the way you think. It changes the way you feel. It changes the way you treat others. It really does. God's Word transforms your life.

Chapter 20

LESS IS MORE!

The cares of this world, and the deceitfulness of riches, and the lusts of other things entering in, choke the word, and it becometh unfruitful.

Mark 4:19

There are so many different things that can come in and take your energy and focus away from the Word of God. There are people who think, *If I could just have more money, I could be a bigger blessing to the church, to the ministry, and to my family. We could get this, we could have that, and we could see these dreams we have come true.* You can go after money if you want, but you're deceived if you think it's going to make you better or happier.

I once read a story about a famous sports figure who used to be number one year after year. In this story, he talked about how empty and desperate he was. This guy had all kinds of fame, money, and everything that comes with it. But those things didn't produce what he wanted. That's the deceit of riches. It's a lie to think, *If I just had more, then I'd be better.* That's not so.

EXACTLY OPPOSITE

You have to stand against the deceitfulness of riches and understand it's only God's Word in your life that is really going to give you the things that count—health, prosperity, relationships, peace, joy, victory—both now and for eternity. You need to understand this and let it sink in to the degree that you make a priority out of God's Word and put it first in everything you do.

> *And these are they which are sown on good ground; such as hear the word, and receive it, and bring forth fruit, some thirtyfold, some sixty, and some an hundred.*

Mark 4:20

This description of the last type of ground really blesses me. Out of all these different kinds of soil, this is the one that was fruitful. What was different about it? What made it so special and productive? It had less. Not more, but less—less rocks, less thorns, less weeds, less of everything that hinders a seed.

When most people start thinking about God using them and His power manifesting in their lives, they automatically say, "I don't have enough education. I don't have enough money. I don't have enough charisma. I don't have enough of this." We think that because we don't have as much as everybody else, God can't use us. But it's exactly opposite in the kingdom of God. Less is more!

NOT JUST FOR PREACHERS!

What makes the Word of God work is your focus and commitment to it. The Word of God will produce in any type of soil if the rocks are taken out, the roots are allowed to grow, the weeds are pulled up, and the choking distractions are taken away. God's Word will work in any believer's heart.

This truth changed my life. I felt like I had everything going against me. I didn't have an education. I'm a hick from Texas. I could hardly talk. I was embarrassed. I couldn't look a person in the face. I was fearful and had nothing going for me. I felt like, *God, I don't have anything to offer You.* But my life was transformed when I saw that the type of ground, or heart, that produces the best results isn't a heart that has more but rather a heart that has less.

So, I responded, "Well, God, I'm not sure I can be more than I am, but I know I can be less. If having less is the key, I can do that. I don't have as much stuff to root out of my life as most people. I don't have any confidence in myself. I've never been a success at anything. I don't have anything tempting me and drawing me away. I can give You my heart for all the rest of my days. I can do that." I just made a decision that I would put God's Word first, and the Word of God has changed my life.

Now, you might say, "Well, Andrew, that's okay for you. You're a preacher, and preachers need to do that." No, I'm telling you that this works for anybody. A friend of mine who is a businessman got hold of the Word of God, and the company he owned began grossing hundreds of millions of dollars per year. His own testimony was that the truths he learned and applied from the Word of God produced this financial prosperity.

I could tell you hundreds of stories of people who have taken the truths of God's Word about forgiveness and turning the other cheek and had relationships restored, marriages healed, and hatred taken out of their hearts (Matt. 5:39). God's Word will work for anybody; it's not just for preachers!

KEEP AFTER IT

Let's look at the parallel verse of Mark 4:20 over in the Gospel of Luke. This verse talks specifically about the type of person in whom the seed brings forth an abundance of fruit:

> *But that on the good ground are they, which in an honest and good heart, having heard the word, keep it, and bring forth fruit with patience.*
>
> **Luke 8:15**

We have to bring forth fruit with patience. This is a missing element in many Christians' lives.

During the conferences we have, some people come at the beginning of the week, and they are pumped. They come expecting to receive, and for a day or two they maintain their excitement. But when they don't see everything they want produced within forty-eight hours, they started battling discouragement and depression.

That's not the way the Word of God works. Now, a person can receive a miracle, and praise God for miracles. But generally speaking, change in the Christian life takes time. And many people just aren't willing to stick with it.

Many who read this book will get excited and spend time for the rest of the week meditating in the Word. Maybe they'll get up early and read God's Word. Or maybe they'll do something to put the Word of God in the forefront, giving it a greater position of importance in their lives. But if they don't see results in a week's time, many will quit.

What would happen if you put a seed in the ground for a week and then dug it up? You'd find that nothing had changed. Do you know what? You aren't ever going to see fruit by doing that. You have to put the seed in the ground, believe by faith that the truths of sowing and reaping work, and just keep it there. Protect it. Water it. Weed around it. Keep after it. And eventually it will produce.

WITH PATIENCE

It's the same way with the Word of God. God's Word doesn't work instantly. In our society, we have instant tea, instant coffee, and instant potatoes, and everyone wants to microwave their miracle. It doesn't come that way. If you're going to receive your miracle from God, you need to take the Word of God, plant it in your heart, and keep on doing that day after day. You need to meditate on it and give the Word time to work. You have to *"bring forth fruit with patience"* (Luke 8:15).

The seed itself didn't determine whether a person got thirtyfold, sixtyfold, or a hundredfold fruit. It wasn't the seed. The seed had the potential to produce a hundredfold in every single situation. The difference was the degree of commitment given to the seed in the person's heart.

There is no difference between you and any other person. And there's no difference between the Word of God in your heart and anyone else's. Your heart is just as capable of producing. The only difference is what you do with it. Does your heart have more? Or less?

> But that on the good ground are they, which in an honest and good heart, having heard the word, keep it, and bring forth fruit with patience.
>
> **Luke 8:15**

Are you going to keep the Word? If you'll do that, God's Word will change your life.

Chapter 21

A CRISIS SITUATION

John the Baptist began to doubt his whole life and faith. How did Jesus deal with those doubts? Through the power of God's Word. The Word is the greatest antidote against doubt and unbelief. This is illustrated in the way Jesus treated John the Baptist.

> *And the disciples of John shewed him of all these things.*
>
> **Luke 7:18**

"These things" is talking about the miracles Jesus performed. The Lord had just commissioned His disciples and sent them out two by two to minister. They started producing miracles—raising the dead, casting out devils, opening blind eyes. So, miracles were happening through Jesus personally and also

through His disciples. These are *"these things"* that John the Baptist's disciples came and showed him.

At this time, John the Baptist had been thrown in prison (Luke 3:19-20). The Bible isn't clear on this, but from what I understand, John only had about a six-month-long ministry. He was so strong and so radical in his statements that he offended Herod the king. That's because Herod married his own sister-in-law, his brother's wife, and John the Baptist openly proclaimed that this was immoral and illegal. So, Herod got mad and put him in prison for at least six months and possibly up to two years.

A MAJOR DEAL!

John the Baptist was in prison and hearing reports of not only Jesus doing all of these miracles but also His disciples. So, John called two of his own disciples and sent them to Jesus, asking, *"Art thou he that should come? or look we for another?"* (Luke 7:19).

Too often we skip over this and don't realize what was happening here. This was John the Baptist doubting whether Jesus was the Christ. He asked, "Are You the Messiah, or should we look for another?" This is a major deal!

John the Baptist wasn't normal like most people would consider normal. He was baptized with the Holy Spirit even while still in his mother's womb (Luke 1:15). He was filled, anointed, and controlled by the Holy Spirit throughout his childhood and growing-up years. He didn't do normal things like in our day and age. He didn't go to school with other kids.

As an only child, he didn't have sibling rivalry. He didn't have a girlfriend or other such interaction. The Word says that John literally went out into the desert and remained there until the day he appeared to the nation of Israel (Luke 1:80).

We don't know for sure, but most people believe John lived with a group of people called the Essenes. These are the people who wrote the Dead Sea Scrolls and put them in those caves. They were a very strict religious order. I've read many things about them and how committed to God they were. For instance, take the Sabbath. The Law says not to do anything on the Sabbath that would be considered work. Well, these Essenes literally had it in their writings that it was against their rules to have a bowel movement on the Sabbath. An Essene could be punished for it. That's how much they controlled themselves! These people were like that, and it seems John was raised by them in the desert.

It wasn't a fun time. John didn't have a natural childhood, and he didn't fall in love. He stayed in the desert for approximately thirty years.

HIS WHOLE LIFE

John's whole life was focused on one thing.

And there appeared unto him an angel of the Lord standing on the right side of the altar of incense. And when Zacharias saw him, he was troubled, and fear fell upon him. But the angel said unto him, Fear not, Zacharias: for thy prayer is heard; and thy wife Elisabeth shall bear thee a son, and thou shalt call his name John. And thou shalt have joy and gladness; and many shall rejoice at his birth. For he shall be great in the sight of the Lord, and shall drink neither wine nor strong drink; and he shall be filled with the Holy Ghost, even from his mother's womb. And many of the children of Israel shall he turn to the Lord their God. And he shall go before him in the spirit and power of Elias, to turn the hearts of the fathers to the children, and the disobedient to the wisdom of the just; to make ready a people prepared for the Lord.

Luke 1:11-17

John's parents had told him about the supernatural, miraculous happenings surrounding his conception and birth. It was prophesied that he would be the one to prepare the way for the Messiah. John the Baptist knew what his purpose was. The Holy Spirit had him focused on this his whole life, with no other pursuits, interests, distractions, or diversions. He was focused on one thing, which was to prepare the way for the Messiah. And at the age of thirty, John just appeared.

In those days came John the Baptist, preaching in the wilderness of Judaea.

Matthew 3:1

John the Baptist didn't show up in the cities, where the people were. The Bible says he went out into the desert. Not many people do that. If someone wants to make an impact today, if they desire to catch fish, they go where the fish are. Not so with John. It was totally miraculous the way he did things. He just walked out into the desert and started preaching to the snakes and scorpions. Maybe some trader came by, heard something, and God touched his heart. He was so moved that he went and got all of his trader friends and brought a whole crowd out. They began to share with others, and pretty soon, within just a six-month period of time, all of the people out of Judea, Samaria, and the regions round about were touched (Mark 1:5, Luke 3:3, and Acts 13:24). Multiple nations were touched by God through a man who wasn't wearing fancy suits. John didn't have a polished demeanor, and he wasn't in the population centers. Instead, he was out in the desert. But in a very short period of time, he stood the world on its ear.

INCREASE AND DECREASE

What was John's message? The message that Jesus is the Christ.

Now when all the people were baptized, it came to pass, that Jesus also being baptized, and praying, the heaven was opened, And the Holy Ghost descended in a bodily shape like a dove upon him, and a voice came from heaven, which said, Thou art my beloved Son; in thee I am well pleased.

Luke 3:21-22

When Jesus walked in front of John, he recognized Him as being the Messiah. John saw the heavens open and the Holy Spirit descending on Jesus as a dove. John heard an audible voice out of heaven declaring, "This is My beloved Son, in whom I am well pleased."

John the Baptist was so convinced that this was the Messiah that he even told his own disciples, including Peter's brother Andrew, to follow Jesus (John 1:29-42).

> *He must increase, but I must decrease.*
>
> **John 3:30**

The scribes and Pharisees came out against John and tried to goad him by saying, "Don't you realize that more people are now following Jesus than are following you?" They were trying to play on his ego to drive a wedge between him and the Lord. John responded, "I told you I wasn't the Messiah. I'm only the messenger in front of Him, not even worthy to stoop down and undo the latch on His sandal" (John 1:26-27). John the Baptist knew that Jesus was the Christ. He publicly stated so four different times.

SEVERE

Yet John is also the same man who had been in prison for at least six months, possibly up to two whole years. And eventually he began doubting whether Jesus was the Christ. It's easy to just read over this quickly and miss the severity of it. But this was severe!

Do you realize what it would have meant to John the Baptist if Jesus wasn't the Christ? This was John's whole life and ministry. His entire life had been given to one purpose, preparing the way for the Messiah. And if Jesus wasn't the Messiah, then John had taken the anointing, the gift on his life, and led multiple nations after the wrong person. This was doubting not only who Jesus was but also who John himself was. John the Baptist's whole life was on the line. This was serious!

For John the Baptist to admit this and to send two of his disciples to Jesus and ask, "Are you the Christ?"—John was in a crisis.

> *When the men were come unto him, they said, John Baptist hath sent us unto thee, saying, Art thou he that should come? or look we for another?*

Luke 7:20

Jesus understood the severity of this. He knew what John was going through. The Lord understood much more than what I've been able to describe to you. Yet how did He respond to John being in this crisis situation?

HIS ANSWER

> *And in that same hour he cured many of their infirmities and plagues, and of evil spirits; and unto many that were blind he gave sight. Then Jesus*

> *answering said unto them, Go your way, and tell*
> *John what things ye have seen and heard; how that*
> *the blind see, the lame walk, the lepers are cleansed,*
> *the deaf hear, the dead are raised, to the poor the*
> *gospel is preached. And blessed is he, whosoever*
> *shall not be offended in me.*

Luke 7:21-23

That was His answer. And the Lord didn't even answer John's disciples directly! He waited about an hour, cured all of kinds of people, and then told John's disciples to go back to John and tell him what they'd seen and heard. Specifically, Jesus wanted them to mention to John that the blind were seeing, the deaf were hearing, the dead were being raised, and the lame were walking, and John would be blessed if he wouldn't be offended in Him. What kind of answer is that?

For many years, when I read this I thought, *Lord, this doesn't seem like an appropriate response to John the Baptist—the guy who opened up the door, drew the crowds, and prepared the way for You to come.* It just doesn't seem like an appropriate response, especially later on when we find out what Jesus really had to say about John (Luke 7:26-28). Why did Jesus compliment John so strongly only *after* his disciples had already left?

The answer to this question is precisely what we're focusing on, which is the importance and the power of the Word of God in your life.

Chapter 22

BACK TO THE WORD!

John the Baptist was in a crisis. He was doubting not only who Jesus was but also who *he* was. If Jesus wasn't the Messiah, then John would be a failure. This was a serious situation!

The Lord gave John's two disciples a seemingly inappropriate answer to deliver to him. Now, this is especially confusing when we read what happened after John's disciples left.

> *And when the messengers of John were departed, he* [Jesus] *began to speak unto the people concerning John.*

> **Luke 7:24a, brackets added**

Once the disciples had left, the Lord complimented John greatly. He didn't do it when the disciples were still within earshot. He didn't say these things so that the messengers would hear them and then go back and tell John. Instead, His message to John was, "Look, the blind eyes are opened, the deaf ears hear, and the lame walk, and you are blessed if you will believe and not be offended."

After John's two disciples departed, Jesus spoke to the people.

> *What went ye out into the wilderness for to see? A reed shaken with the wind?*

Luke 7:24b

WET CAMEL'S HAIR

This is a sarcastic statement. Of course the people didn't go out into the desert to see a reed shaking in the wind. Besides, reeds grow more around water, not in the desert. It wasn't the beautiful scenery that drew all the people out there.

> *But what went ye out for to see? A man clothed in soft raiment? Behold, they which are gorgeously apparelled, and live delicately, are in kings' courts.*

Luke 7:25

This was another sarcastic statement. Jesus was basically saying, "What drew you out into the desert? John the Baptist's fancy clothing? Certainly not!" Clothed with camel hair, this guy must have been a sight. I remember reading somewhere that the only thing that smells worse than camel's hair is wet camel's hair. John was constantly in the water baptizing people, so this guy probably stank! He had long hair, and the locusts and honey he ate probably stuck to his bushy beard. This guy was a character (Matt. 3:4)!

> *But what went ye out for to see? A prophet? Yea, I say unto you, and much more than a prophet. This is he, of whom it is written, Behold, I send my messenger before thy face, which shall prepare thy way before thee. For I say unto you, Among those that are born of women there is not a greater prophet than John the Baptist: but he that is least in the kingdom of God is greater than he.*
>
> Luke 7:26-28

These words that Jesus spoke about John the Baptist being the greatest prophet ever put him in a category above Moses, Elijah, Isaiah, King David, Solomon—really anybody you could mention. But if John the Baptist was experiencing doubt and needed reassurance, why didn't the Lord say all these things to his disciples before sending them back?

DON'T QUIT—HOLD ON!

Jesus was the most influential man in that part of the world at that time. Those who had heard about Jesus were forsaking jobs, families, and everything to come out and hear Him. Jesus was seeing the blind healed, the dead raised, and all kinds of miracles. He was the center of attention. He had more influence than anybody. What would it have done for John the Baptist if Jesus—the most important man on the face of the earth—had said, "John the Baptist is the greatest man who has ever lived up until this period of time"? Do you know what? That would have stoked John's fire. That would have blessed and excited him.

I remember a time in my own life when I wasn't seeing the turnout at my meetings that I knew God wanted me to have. We were struggling financially. I was doing everything I knew to do, and it just didn't seem like things were working.

So, I went to a conference at Calvary Cathedral in Fort Worth, Texas, where Bob Nichols pastors. I really appreciate Bob and his wife, Joy. Bob is a great friend of mine and serves on my board of directors. But back then, I had only met him one time previously, and it was a very negative situation. A neighbor had wanted to get the two of us together, but I wouldn't impose on this man's friendship with Bob to meet him. So, I told him no. Finally, this guy invited both Bob and me over to his house for supper, and he didn't tell either of us that anybody else was going to be there. When Bob and I arrived, my neighbor threw us together, locked us in a room, and tried to make us fellowship. Bob was very gracious and kind to me, but I was super embarrassed. It was just a negative meeting, and I thought that if Bob Nichols ever heard my name again, he'd go the other direction.

That was the only contact I'd ever had with Bob Nichols before going to his church for a conference. All of the big-name speakers were there—like Kenneth Copeland and Kenneth Hagin—and these guys were prophesying to each other. They were getting all kinds of awesome words from the Lord. I remember sitting right in the middle of my row, something like ten seats in from the aisle, in that huge auditorium full of people. During the song service they said, "Go around and greet someone." I was feeling so small and insignificant, and I thought, *God, I need help. I need somebody to encourage me.* It was similar to how John the Baptist must have been feeling. I don't believe it was near that bad, but it was similar. And I was praying for help.

Do you know what happened? Bob Nichols, the pastor of that church, somehow spotted me out of that crowd of two thousand people, got off the platform, ran back to where I was in the middle of this row, and started hugging me. This wasn't convenient. He excused himself and pushed himself through all of these folks, came up to me, wrapped his arms around me, and wouldn't let go. It wasn't just a little charismatic hug. He started saying, "Brother, I love you. God loves you. Don't quit. Hold on!" And he wouldn't let go of me. He just held me and ministered to me. Then he went back up to the front of the auditorium.

SCROLLS

Do you know what that did? It encouraged me. It blessed me to think that this well-known man who was hosting this whole conference singled me out and ministered to me. He didn't have to do that. I took it as an expression of God's love for me, and it really ministered to me.

As I read this story about John the Baptist, I thought, *Jesus, why didn't You say all of these compliments about John while his messengers were still there so they could hear it too?* To me, it just didn't seem like He gave John what he needed. I just didn't understand this passage of Scripture for a long time. In fact, when I would read this, it would actually upset me. I would think, *God, I just don't understand this. I don't relate to it.*

Then one day I was reading Isaiah 40:3-5:

> *The voice of him that crieth in the wilderness, Prepare ye the way of the LORD, make straight in the desert a highway for our God. Every valley shall be exalted, and every mountain and hill shall be made low: and the crooked shall be made straight, and the rough places plain: And the glory of the LORD shall be revealed, and all flesh shall see it together: for the mouth of the LORD hath spoken it.*

These are scriptures that John the Baptist was familiar with. They were written on scrolls and not in chapters and verses like today. For John to have quoted from the above passage (which he did in Luke 3:4-6) means that he knew the book of Isaiah completely.

> *Strengthen ye the weak hands, and confirm the feeble knees. Say to them that are of a fearful heart, Be*

strong, fear not: behold, your God will come with vengeance, even God with a recompence; he will come and save you. Then the eyes of the blind shall be opened, and the ears of the deaf shall be unstopped. Then shall the lame man leap as an hart, and the tongue of the dumb sing: for in the wilderness shall waters break out, and streams in the desert.

Isaiah 35:3-6

"I FULFILLED THE PROPHECIES"

As I was reading this prophecy one day about the Messiah to come, it dawned on me that the messenger who prepared the way for the Messiah would have known these scriptures. Then, all of a sudden, the Holy Spirit reminded me that this is what Jesus told John's disciples to go back and tell him.

Then Jesus answering said unto them, Go your way, and tell John what things ye have seen and heard; how that the blind see, the lame walk, the lepers are cleansed, the deaf hear, the dead are raised, to the poor the gospel is preached. And blessed is he, whosoever shall not be offended in me.

Luke 7:22-23

Instead of John simply getting some kind of a kudo from Jesus that would bless him for a day or a week, Jesus sent John back to the very scriptures that prophesied what would happen when the Messiah came. These scriptures said that when that happened, the eyes of the blind would be opened, the ears of the deaf would be unstopped, and the lame man would leap as a deer (Is. 35:5-6).

> *And in that same hour he cured many of their infirmities and plagues, and of evil spirits; and unto many that were blind he gave sight. Then Jesus answering said unto them, Go your way, and tell John what things ye have seen and heard; how that the blind see, the lame walk, the lepers are cleansed, the deaf hear, the dead are raised, to the poor the gospel is preached.*
>
> **Luke 7:21-22**

Jesus went out in the same hour and healed people who were blind, lame, and deaf. And He threw in raising someone from the dead as a bonus. Do you realize what Christ did? He fulfilled Isaiah 35:5-6. He didn't ignore John's messengers. He didn't take John's cry for help lightly. Jesus fulfilled the Word of God in a miraculous fashion, for He fulfilled it all in *one hour*. He did it all in a short period of time and threw in the raising of the dead so nobody would mistakenly think everything else was just a coincidence.

Jesus basically told John's disciples, "Go back and tell John what you saw and heard. I fulfilled the prophecies" (Luke 7:22). The Lord sent John the Baptist back to the Word!

Chapter 23

A SICK HEART

Hope deferred maketh the heart sick: but when the desire cometh, it is a tree of life.

Proverbs 13:12

John the Baptist knew he was called by God to prepare the way for the Messiah. And if John was like everyone else in his day, he viewed the first and second coming of the Lord as one single event. Jesus even referenced Isaiah 61:1-2 when He declared:

> *The Spirit of the Lord is upon me, because he hath anointed me to preach the gospel to the poor; he hath sent me to heal the brokenhearted, to preach deliverance to the captives, and recovering of sight*

> *to the blind, to set at liberty them that are bruised,*
> *To preach the acceptable year of the Lord.*

Luke 4:18-19

But notice where Jesus ended this passage in Luke. Isaiah 61:2 adds the phrase *"and the day of vengeance of our God."*

We now know that Jesus came to bring in the New Covenant and to preach the Gospel, and there has now been at least a two-thousand-year church age between the first and second advents of the Lord. But in the Old Testament scriptures, the advents kind of ran together. The church age wasn't real distinct or pronounced. So, the people in Jesus's day were constantly expecting to see the Messiah not only come and make an atonement for sin but also set up His physical kingdom. They were also looking for Him to rule with a rod of iron and destroy all opposition. The Jewish nation expected deliverance from Roman rule and for their king—the Messiah—to begin reigning over and controlling the whole earth.

FALSE EXPECTATIONS

John the Baptist knew he was called by God to prepare the way for the Messiah. At one time, he believed fully, completely, and with zero reservation that Jesus was the Messiah. But after John had suffered six months to two years in prison, Christ was still doing no more than healing people, performing miracles, and preaching about having a relationship with God. John wasn't seeing Jesus counter the Roman authority or establish a physical kingdom. As a matter of fact, the Lord was teaching just the opposite.

> *But I say unto you, That ye resist not evil: but who-soever shall smite thee on thy right cheek, turn to him the other also.*

Matthew 5:39

Like everyone else, John had false expectations, and hope deferred makes the heart sick (Prov. 13:12). That's why we need to make sure that when we're hoping for something, it's really a God-ordained deal. John the Baptist was sitting in prison probably expecting Jesus to overthrow the Roman government, liberate the Jews from foreign occupation, and begin to rule the world. Perhaps he was even expecting that this would also cause his own release from prison. Because this wasn't happening, John started having doubts.

This same thing happens all the time. For instance, if a person genuinely expects to be promoted at their job within six months, but two years pass by, I can guarantee that some doubts would begin popping up. Maybe they'd think, *Did God really lead me to this job? What's happening here?* Hope deferred makes the heart sick.

FANTASY AND ENTERTAINMENT

When John the Baptist began to doubt whether Jesus was really the Messiah, he sent two of his own disciples to ask Him about it. The Lord paid all kinds of compliments to John, but not until after these two messengers had already left. Christ's answer didn't seem appropriate to me, and I puzzled over this for many years. Finally, the Lord showed me what He really did. Instead of ignoring or shunning John the Baptist when he had a problem, Jesus gave him His very best, which was the Word. Jesus fulfilled Scripture. In the presence of these two messengers, in one hour's time, He fulfilled all these prophecies from Isaiah 35:5-6. Then He told John's disciples to go back and tell John what they had seen.

When they did, I believe John was immediately reminded of these prophecies concerning the Messiah in Isaiah 35:5-6. The Holy Spirit quickened to him that Jesus was the Messiah because He fulfilled the requirements.

What do you think would have blessed John the Baptist the most? His disciples returning and saying, "Jesus, the most influential man on the face of the earth, said that you are the greatest person who has ever been born up until this point in history"? Would that have been better than having proof that the Scripture is true and that Jesus is the Messiah because He fulfilled it (Luke 7:20-23)?

As touchy, feely, and emotional as we are today, most of us would answer, "Well, I'd like those nice things to be said about me." But you know, emotion from such things wears off. This is one of the major problems in our society today. We just always want to feel good. We don't care if it's right or not. We just want to feel a certain way. So, we immerse ourselves in fantasy and entertainment that isn't based on reality just to get this feeling of contentment.

MOTIVATED AND DIRECTED

We need to recognize that truth is more powerful than emotions. If Jesus had just given John the Baptist some kind of a feeling, it would have worn off. And the next week, John's messengers would have been right back there saying, "John's lost his goose bumps. Can You say something else that will really make him feel good?" But see, John was rooted. He grew up on the Word of God. He knew the Word. When he was asked questions by the scribes and Pharisees, he quoted from God's Word. The Word was what motivated him and directed his life. So, when John began to doubt, what did Jesus do? He put him back on the Word of God. I simply cannot overemphasize how important this is.

Other than a few exceptions, most of the time I don't get prophecies. I could go to a meeting, and every person on my row could get a prophecy, but I'd be the one who got skipped over. At first, it bothered me. I wondered, *God, what's the matter? Is something wrong with me? How come I don't get prophecies and words of knowledge and wisdom?* Do you know what He told me? He said, "My highest is to deal with you by the Word, letting you believe My Word. That is the strongest, greatest realm of faith that you can get into. I can deal with you on a lower level, but it's because I want you to walk in My best that I'm not giving you those things."

Now, don't misunderstand what I'm saying. I'm not trying to criticize dreams, visions, prophecies, and the like. There have been times when I've experienced those things, but it's not often. And the Lord has tried to move me beyond that. Those are for when you're struggling. But the stronger you get in the Lord, the more He wants you to walk by faith.

STRUGGLING

This is the reason Jesus responded to John the Baptist the way He did. It wasn't because He didn't respect him, but because He respected him so much. Jesus said:

> *For I say unto you, Among those that are born of women there is not a greater prophet than John the Baptist: but he that is least in the kingdom of God is greater than he.*

Luke 7:28

What a tremendous statement! Jesus respected John the Baptist. He respected him so much that He didn't want to just stroke him emotionally and give him some kind of a feeling that would be temporary and wear off. Instead, He referred him back to the Word.

That's what God wants to do in your life too. Maybe you're struggling with doubt. Maybe you're wondering about your purpose or about everything that you feel God has called you to do. You're just looking for some kind of a feeling. You're praying for a dream. You're wanting some person to come and do something. What you need to do is go back to God's Word and hear His voice speak to you through His Word. That's what will change your life.

Chapter 24

FEED YOUR FAITH

When John the Baptist doubted, Jesus pointed him back to the Word. This is what the Lord wants to do in our lives too. He wants us to put more emphasis on the truth of the Word of God rather than on circumstances, feelings, or confirmations.

So many people want the Lord to speak to them through two visions, three dreams, and four prophecies to confirm something. Of course, everyone is responsible to God on their own. But for me, that's just not the way I function. If the Word of God speaks something to me, that settles it. I don't care if a dream, vision, or anybody's prophecy says something contrary. In fact, I've had prophecies, dreams, and visions that were completely opposite of what God told me.

As a young man, I had two dreams that I thought were demonic. So, I began rebuking them. Then a woman walked up to me in a restaurant that was three hundred miles away from where I lived. I didn't know anyone there, and this woman came up to me out of the blue and said, "God speaks once, yea twice, in visions and dreams of the night, when deep sleep falls upon men," which is a reference to Job 33:14-15. Then she told me that I had been rebuking those dreams because I'd thought that they were from the devil, but they were actually from God. Instantly fear and panic came all over me. I wondered, *How could this be?* So, I seriously started considering submitting to those dreams. Basically, they were about my total destruction and that I would become an invalid.

A little while later a man came across my path who said that God had given him seven incurable diseases. This was back when I was first getting started and wasn't very established in the truth that God is a good God and doesn't do that. So, I was beginning to believe these dreams and this prophecy. Then here came this minister, who was well respected in some circles, with all these diseases. He preached that God did this to him.

I went out to eat with this minister, and someone I was with told him about the two dreams and the woman coming in and giving me that prophecy. This man began to prophesy and say, "You're going to be a human vegetable for eight years. You'll be brain dead and kept alive on machines only. Then after you come out of this, you'll be stronger than ever before." I was so weak in the Lord that I almost accepted this. My attitude was, "Lord, if this is what You have for me, I'm willing to do it." I was a hairsbreadth away from humbling myself and saying, "I receive it."

OVERPLAYED HIS HAND

At that time, I had an incurable disease. Right before my wife and I were married, I was diagnosed with yellow jaundice, which couldn't be cured. I was told that if I lay still in bed for like six weeks, my body would recover. But if I didn't lie still, and continued living normally, it could kill me. Anyway, all these things were happening, and I was thinking, *Well, maybe this is the way it's going to happen. I'll just continue pouring concrete for a living like I do, and this illness will come over me.*

I was so close to submitting to all of this stuff, but the devil overplayed his hand like he always does. This minister came out and said, "The worst part about all this isn't having to suffer with these diseases or face death every day; it's that God has closed His Word to me. For eight years now, I never open the Bible unless I'm preaching. I never study. God won't let me study the Word. He's shut me off from His Word."

Boy, that did it. I didn't know much, but I knew God would not close His Word to me. I knew the promises in the Word of God and how important it is to feed on the Word daily.

I remember standing up in the restaurant in front of this respected guest minister, the pastor of the church, and all the leaders—I was barely twenty at this time—and saying, "You're all wrong. I don't care what you say. God will never shut His Word to me." I renounced the whole thing, walked out, and left that church. I believe it saved me from that stuff coming to pass. We need to submit to God and resist the devil (James 4:7). And it's God's Word that helps us do that.

Some people want to base things on visions and dreams. If a vision or dream confirms what God has already said to me through His Word, I'll accept it. But if a vision, dream, or even an angel comes to me and says anything contrary to God's Word, I'm not accepting it (Gal. 1:8-9). I've been through this type of thing more than once.

DRIVE OUT DOUBT

So many people are looking for these other things. They come up to me and ask, "Brother, do you have a word for me?" Yet their Bible is right there, tucked under their arm. I want to say, "There are thousands of words from God to you right there. That's the Lord speaking to you!" But most people don't take the Bible as being the infallible Word of God. They just think it vaguely represents Him, and they use it sparingly, pulling out a verse as they walk out the door. Most people haven't based their lives on the Word. They haven't committed themselves to it.

Most of us would have opted for what Jesus said about John the Baptist in Luke 7:28: "Boy, you're the most important person who has ever lived on the face of the earth." We would rather have had that than have Christ fulfill a scripture and say, "Believe or don't believe." However, Jesus respected John so much that He referred him back to the Word (Luke 7:22-23).

Are you struggling with doubt in any area of your life today? You don't need some type of an emotional experience. You don't need a prophecy, a vision, or a dream. What you need is to get back into the Word of God.

So then faith cometh by hearing, and hearing by the word of God.

Romans 10:17

Faith will drive doubt and unbelief out of our lives. We've made the Christian life too hard. We think it's so difficult to serve God. Well, it's only hard if we aren't meditating in the Word. The Bible says that if we meditate in the Word day and night, then we will have good success and we will make our way prosperous.

SIMPLE AND TRUE

This book of the law shall not depart out of thy mouth; but thou shalt meditate therein day and night, that thou mayest observe to do according to all that is written therein: for then thou shalt make thy way prosperous, and then thou shalt have good success.

Joshua 1:8

Notice that it doesn't say you *might* make your way prosperous; it says you *will*. Putting God's Word first place in your life will automatically produce everything you need. It will just come effortlessly.

Have you ever seen a tree groan, moan, shake, and then—*boom*—there's an apple? That's not the way fruit comes. It's just the nature of that tree to produce apples, but it takes time. And it takes being an apple tree all of the time. It takes consistency. You have to stay planted. You have to stay rooted. You can't ever move. If you stay right there in the Word, you'll just automatically produce fruit.

This is what we must learn in the Christian life. God wants His Word to be the foundation of everything we do. The reason most people aren't having more success is because they haven't put priority on the Word of God the way that they should. That's simple, but it's true.

THE GREATER BLESSING

Earlier we looked at how Jesus marveled at the centurion's faith (Matt. 8:10). Jesus called it *"great."* The centurion said, *"Speak the Word only."* He understood the power and authority of the Word of God (Matt. 8:5-13).

Thomas, known as the doubter, said that he wouldn't believe until he had seen and touched (John 20:19-29). Jesus told him, "Thomas, there's a greater blessing on those who believe without seeing, without physical evidence." God's Word is the evidence.

Do you want the greater blessing? Would you like to walk in great faith? Then believe the report of the Lord. It's recorded for you in God's Word.

Go ahead, feed your faith and starve your doubts!

Chapter 25

TWO DOORS

John the Baptist—the greatest prophet to have ever walked on the earth prior to Jesus—experienced doubt. He sent a couple of his disciples to Jesus to ask Him if He really was the Christ. Basically, John was asking the Lord to help remove his doubt. He wanted to believe. He had already professed publicly that Jesus was the Christ. But John was struggling with doubt. The Lord helped him by referring him back to the Word (Luke 7:22-23).

After John's disciples left, Jesus complimented John greatly. Most of us would opt for the compliments over the Word any day. If there were two doors in front of us, one labeled "Feelings" and the other "Fact," most of us would go for the feelings.

I remember listening to an audiocassette once where a woman was dealing with a girl who had terrible anger and resentment problems toward her parents. The woman on the tape said that she knew the girl's parents and knew that they had done nothing wrong, had never abused this girl, and had always loved her. But because this girl's parents had a strict standard and didn't want their daughter to use drugs, drink alcohol, or have premarital sex the way that other kids did, the girl interpreted this as her parents being restrictive, not loving her, etc. This woman on the tape admitted that even though what this girl was feeling about her parents wasn't accurate, it was accurate to the girl because she *felt* it. So, this woman went ahead and ministered to the girl about forgiving her parents and learning how to let it go.

When I heard this, I had a flesh flash. I got so mad that I yanked that tape out of the player and threw it out the window. Although I don't recommend doing that, the whole situation just infuriated me. Even though this woman knew that the girl's perception wasn't reality, she chose to deal with it as if it *were*, just because the girl "felt" like it was. In a sense, that's putting feelings over truth.

I would have said, "Hey, you have misinterpreted all of this. You think that just because your parents said no to something, they're against you. That's not it at all." I'd try to get rid of the root of this thing, because even if this girl received ministry, felt better, and forgave her parents, something else would come up again later on. Somebody else would tell her no, she'd be denied something she wanted in life, and she'd never deal with the root of the problem, which was her own self-centeredness and blindness.

FEELINGS OR FACT

As long as you go through life thinking everybody else is your problem, you're never going to be free of problems. It doesn't matter what other people do; it matters how you respond to it. When you understand that, you can start receiving and walking in liberty.

With the choice between two doors, "Feelings" or "Fact," most people would choose the first. We desire to feel good more than we desire truth. That's why when we're dealing with a person who is expressing doubt—and having the emotional trauma that goes along with it—most of us would just put our arms around them and try to make them feel something. But that wasn't the approach of Jesus. The Lord referred John the Baptist back to the Word (Luke 7:22-23). He gave him the truth (John 14:6 and 17:17).

For you to deal with your doubts, to succeed in life, and to overcome all of the things that come your way, you're going to have to get past just wanting, praying for, and needing somebody to come along every time you need a little boost. Please don't misunderstand what I'm saying. There are times when everyone needs help. You aren't an island, so don't be too proud to receive. But I am encouraging you to get past the place of always expecting it. Don't make your life codependent upon everybody else doing what's right and always saying nice things about you. Go to the Word of God and let God's Word be your foundation.

Moreover I will endeavour that ye may be able after my decease to have these things always in remembrance. For we have not followed cunningly devised fables, when we made known unto you the power and coming of our Lord Jesus Christ, but were eyewitnesses of his majesty. For he received from God the Father honour and glory, when there came such a voice to him from the excellent glory, This is my beloved Son, in whom I am well pleased. And this voice which came from heaven we heard, when we were with him in the holy mount.

2 Peter 1:15-18

Peter was saying, "I'm endeavoring to write these things down so that after I die, you will still have a record of what I've told you." Why did he want to do this? Peter told us why: "Because we haven't spoken to you about things we've devised. These aren't fables or fairy tales. This is reality. This Word that we have told you about, the things we've seen and heard—they are real." Peter was just trying to validate his message.

SHEKINAH GLORY

It would be similar to me coming to your town and going on the radio, television, and social media and saying, "God has appeared to me. I had three angels, two dreams, and a prophecy. Meet me at the hotel ballroom downtown and I'll tell you the things God has spoken to me." If I were to promote that and really hype it up, the hotel wouldn't be able to handle the number of folks who would attend. People would come by the thousands to hear somebody who had just had God appear to them and give them a specific word for their city.

This is what the Apostle Peter was doing in Second Peter 1:16-18. He said, "Hey, the things I've been telling you—these things aren't made up." Then he made reference to a miraculous encounter he had personally experienced:

> *And after six days Jesus taketh Peter, James, and John his brother, and bringeth them up into an high mountain apart, And was transfigured before them: and his face did shine as the sun, and his raiment was white as the light. And, behold, there appeared unto them Moses and Elias talking with him. Then answered Peter, and said unto Jesus, Lord, it is good for us to be here: if thou wilt, let us make here three tabernacles; one for thee, and one for Moses, and one for Elias. While he yet spake, behold, a bright cloud overshadowed them: and behold a voice out of the cloud, which said, This is my beloved Son, in whom I am well pleased; hear ye him. And when the disciples heard it, they fell on their face, and were sore afraid. And Jesus came and touched them, and said, Arise, and be not afraid. And when they had lifted up their eyes, they saw no man, save Jesus only.*

Matthew 17:1-8

Jesus took three of His disciples—Peter, James, and John—and they all went up onto a mountain, and Christ was transfigured before them. He literally started radiating light. When Peter saw this, he fell on his face. Then Peter also saw Moses and Elijah talking with Jesus, conversing with Him about what would happen at His crucifixion. When Peter saw this, he wanted to build three tabernacles. About that time, a cloud overshadowed them—the shekinah glory of God—and an audible voice came out of that cloud. This is the example Peter was referring to in Second Peter 1.

MIRACULOUS EVENTS

Peter was saying, "I know what I'm telling you is true. I know Jesus is the Christ because I saw Him magnified. I saw Him literally radiate light. He didn't reflect it the way Moses did. He radiated—light came out of Him. I saw the shekinah glory of God that used to overshadow and indwell the temple. I saw that. I heard God the Father speak audibly from heaven." Why was Peter referring to all these miraculous events? Here's why: "To validate that the message I'm preaching to you is true. Jesus is the Christ. I know it because of these miraculous things."

But then look what he said next:

We have also a more sure word of prophecy.

2 Peter 1:19a

This is an amazing statement. Like I stated earlier, if I came to your town and declared "God appeared to me; I've had this vision, this dream," people would turn out by the thousands. But what if I came and said, "God has spoken to me through His Word. He's taught me truths from His Word that have changed my life, and they could change yours too. Come to this meeting"? Do you know what? Not as many people would come, because not as many people put as much emphasis, value, and worth on the Word of God as they do a vision, an angel, or a dream. But Peter was saying, "We have a more sure word of prophecy."

What could be surer than seeing Jesus transfigured? Or seeing Moses, Elijah, and the shekinah glory of God? Or hearing the audible voice of the Father? What could beat that?

> *Knowing this first, that no prophecy of the scripture is of any private interpretation. For the prophecy came not in old time by the will of man: but holy men of God spake as they were moved by the Holy Ghost.*
>
> **2 Peter 1:20-21**

Do you know what Peter was saying? He was saying, "We have something even better than these things I've told you about, and that's the Word of God. The Word of God confirms that Jesus is the Christ." That's awesome! That rings my bell.

GOD'S SYSTEM

Many people just don't think the Word of God is that important. If there were two doors in front of you, one labeled "The Word of God" and the other "Visions and Dreams," most people would want the key to the one with dreams, visions, and other miraculous stuff. But if you would get hold of the Word of God, if you would begin to make that the foundation of your life and base your life on the Word, that's what would change you. That is God's system. As a matter of fact, the reason you don't have more visions, dreams, and physical manifestations is because you couldn't handle it. You have to be mature in the Word of God to really be able to handle those kinds of things.

The greatest gift God has given us, outside of our personal salvation, is a physical copy of the Word of God. And the Holy Spirit will interpret it to us and make it come alive on the inside of us. The Word is the greatest gift we could ever have, and most of us just aren't fully appreciating it.

Chapter 26

TRAIN YOUR MIND

The Word of God is the foundation of any successful Christian life. If you're really going to prosper, you have to know the Word of God—not know something about it. You shouldn't just be saying, "Well, the pastor said it's God's will to heal." You need to get into God's Word for yourself. God's Word needs to speak to you. You need to know these things directly from God.

As Peter revealed, God's Word is *"a more sure word of prophecy"* (2 Pet. 1:19).

Peter knew that the message he had was true because he saw Jesus glorified, heard an audible voice from God, and saw Moses and Elijah in the spirit talking to the Lord. Then Peter went on to say, "I have something even greater than that." Believers have the written Word of God!

GOOSE BUMPS

If you would rather have goose bumps that are associated with some physical manifestation than have the assurance that comes from God's Word, then you have a problem in your life. You really do. I'm not saying this to hurt you but rather to point out that most people have not placed the proper value on God's Word. How much time are you spending in the Word of God now that you're almost finished reading this book? How much time do you invest really studying the Word of God?

I'm aware that we go through seasons in our lives. I'll often share that when I was a soldier in Vietnam, I spent sixteen hours a day for thirteen months studying the Word of God. That's true, and it made a huge impact on my life. But now I can't spend sixteen hours a day in the Word. As a matter of fact, if I were to spend sixteen hours a day reading the Bible, I'd be going against what God told me to do. There are different seasons in each of our lives.

If you are in a period of your life where you can just shut yourself off and be with God in the Word, more power to you. It's not going to hurt you. It would do nothing but help you. I'm not saying you have to spend sixteen hours a day studying the Word, but you do have to spend time in it.

Then, once you've read and studied the Scripture, one of the greatest things you can do is meditate in it. You don't have to spend more than twenty or thirty minutes in the Word to be able to get enough material to meditate on for days or weeks. This is how I spend a lot of my time in the Word.

I probably average more than an hour or two a day studying the Word. I also listen to audio recordings while driving. I'm constantly meditating on the Word, and to me, that's being in the Word.

WORRY IS MEDITATION

Did you know that the early New Testament church didn't have a Bible like we do now? They did have the Old Testament scriptures, but those scriptures were contained in large scrolls and confined primarily to the synagogues. The average Christian didn't have a copy of Scripture, yet they stayed in the Word constantly. How did they do it? By continually meditating on the things that Jesus said. The very first disciples didn't even have a copy of what the Lord had said. They just focused on Him, spent more time praying, and let the Holy Spirit bring back to mind the things that Jesus had said. That was being in the Word.

You don't have to have the Bible open and be reading it to be in the Word. By keeping your mind stayed upon the Lord and communicating with Him in your heart through your thoughts, you're in the Word. You're meditating on Scripture.

Now, there are times that you need to pull out some dictionaries, concordances, and other reference tools to dig into the Word and find out what it's really saying. When the Lord shows me things, I go to a number of different versions of the Bible and look those things up. I spend half an hour to an hour looking things up, but then I spend two or three hours sitting back and thinking about what I just read. I don't even have my

Bible open. I just think about what I read, letting the truths and thoughts sink down on the inside of me. That's being in the Word of God.

I just want to be sure to counter any remaining misconceptions. I've been putting such an importance on the Word that you might think, *Well, I can't be in the Word of God twenty-four hours a day. I just can't fulfill this.* It may seem overwhelming, and you may be tempted to just give up. But the truth is, you can meditate constantly. In fact, you do meditate constantly. You may not know it, but you do.

Worry is nothing but meditating on something negative that might happen. Usually people worry about something that hasn't even come to pass yet. They can do many different activities—work, drive, take the kids to school, clean house, have the kids at home—and yet never get that worry out of their hearts and minds. Worry is meditation.

FLIP-FLOPPED

In the same way that you can keep your mind stayed on negative things, you can also keep your mind stayed on positive things. You really can (Phil. 4:6-9). One of the ways that I love to be with the Lord is to get in my vehicle, plug in a praise or teaching CD, and just drive. I'll drive for hours and meditate on things that God is speaking to me. If I'm really focused on something that the Lord is saying and I'm receiving direction about something specific, I'll usually put on a worship CD so that I don't have to focus my attention on a teaching. I'll just sing along with the praise and worship while my mind meditates on God and what He's speaking to me. I have a tremendous time, and that's being in the Word.

You may not be able to spend hour upon hour just sitting there reading the Word, but you can meditate in it. However, you can't meditate on something you don't know.

If you are just getting started, then what I've just described isn't going to be that functional for you. As a matter of fact, my life has nearly flip-flopped. When I first started seeking the Lord, I would spend sixteen hours a day just reading the Word because I didn't know what it said. Even though I might have read through it and heard references, I didn't know the context of different verses and passages. I wasn't familiar enough with it that I could bring all of those statements back to my mind just by memory.

So, if you are brand new to this, then you may have to start by going off somewhere alone and taking every available moment to start reading the Word of God. After you get to know some things, you can increase the amount of time you spend in the Word by just beginning to keep your mind stayed on God and meditating on it over and over again. That's where the real power is released.

COUNTERPRODUCTIVE

When I was spending sixteen hours a day in the Word, I didn't have the Word of God producing in my life nearly as well as I do now. The Word of God is working better in my life today than it was all those years ago when I was spending sixteen hours a day in it.

Now, I'm not discrediting just sitting there and studying the Word. I'm saying it's about how much of the Word you know and how much you're applying it to your life. When I go to the office, I keep my mind stayed on the Lord. I fellowship with Him. I've gotten to where I can keep my mind in tune with God and listen to Him. Ultimately, this is what you need to do. God's Word has to become your foundation.

I know that what I'm saying may seem out of reach for you right now, but you can do it.

> *For though we walk in the flesh, we do not war after the flesh: (For the weapons of our warfare are not carnal, but mighty through God to the pulling down of strong holds;) Casting down imaginations, and every high thing that exalteth itself against the knowledge of God, and bringing into captivity every thought to the obedience of Christ.*
>
> **2 Corinthians 10:3-5**

Notice that it says to bring every thought into captivity. Every thought! You can literally get to where every thought you have is captive to God and His Word. You might be saying, "That can't happen." Well, don't wake me up, because it's working for me. It *can* happen, and that's exactly what this scripture passage reveals.

That's the potential we have, but it doesn't happen without effort. We have to train our minds to be stayed upon the things of God. And the way that many of us watch television and do other things is counterproductive to this. But it can be done.

FOCUSED

This is where the benefit comes in:

> *Thou wilt keep him in perfect peace, whose mind is stayed on thee: because he trusteth in thee.*
>
> **Isaiah 26:3**

Meditating in the Word of God is a way to train your mind to stay focused on Him.

> *For to be carnally minded is death; but to be spiritually minded is life and peace.*
>
> **Romans 8:6**

What is carnal-mindedness? It's not having all of your thoughts stayed on God. But to be spiritually minded—or God-and-His-Word-minded—is life and peace.

Life, peace, fellowship, stability, and fruitfulness—all these and more will be yours in ever-increasing measure as you build your life upon the sure foundation of God's Word!

THE LAST WORD

The truths I've shared with you in this book have changed my life, and I know they will change yours too if you receive them and act on them.

The Lord has shown me thousands of truths that have set me and others free. But all of those truths came through the revelation of His Word. I can truthfully say that if it weren't for God's Word and the Holy Spirit giving me revelation of His Word, my life would be a wreck. My son would not be alive today. I would not have a granddaughter. I would still be an introvert. I would never have survived some of the things life has thrown my way. I certainly would not have fulfilled the ministry God had planned for me.

The impact of God's Word on my life is the single most important thing that has happened to me beyond being born again and baptized in the Holy Spirit. In fact, I would not have been born again or walked in the power of the Holy Spirit without God's Word.

First Peter 1:23 says that we are born again through the incorruptible seed (*spora/sperma*) of God's Word. Everything that pertains to life and godliness comes to us through God's Word (2 Pet. 1:3-4).

I challenge you to make the study of God's Word a priority in your life. The devil will try to steal God's Word from you through persecution and/or busyness that will choke God's Word and keep it from producing. But in the end, you have the final say. The devil cannot make any of those things work without your consent and cooperation.

If you don't know where or how to start, I suggest you start with the scriptures I've used in this book. Look them up in your Bible, and put them in their context. Meditate on them, and ask the Lord to make these truths yours. Let them take root in you.

Then start reading in the Gospels. You need a good understanding of the New Covenant before you get into the Old Testament. I also encourage you to get teaching materials from seasoned ministers whose lives show the evidence of a true minister of God's Word (Mark 16:20).

You can call our Helpline at 719-635-1111 to get further direction, or you can go to our website: **awmi.net**.

I pray that the words I've spoken to you in this book have burned in your heart and ignited a fire that will never be put out.

The best is yet to come!

Andrew Wommack

RECEIVE JESUS
AS YOUR SAVIOR

Choosing to receive Jesus Christ as your Lord and Savior is the most important decision you'll ever make!

God's Word promises that *"if thou shalt confess with thy mouth the Lord Jesus, and shalt believe in thine heart that God hath raised him from the dead, thou shalt be saved. For with the heart man believeth unto righteousness; and with the mouth confession is made unto salvation"* (Rom. 10:9-10). *"For whosoever shall call upon the name of the Lord shall be saved"* (Rom. 10:13).

By His grace, God has already done everything to provide salvation. Your part is simply to believe and receive.

Pray out loud, "Jesus, I confess that You are my Lord and Savior. I believe in my heart that God raised You from the dead. By faith in Your Word, I receive salvation now. Thank You for saving me!"

The very moment you commit your life to Jesus Christ, the truth of His Word instantly comes to pass in your spirit. Now that you're born again, there's a brand-new you!

Please contact our Helpline (719-635-1111) and let us know that you've prayed to receive Jesus as your Savior. We would like to rejoice with you and help you understand more fully what has taken place in your life. We'll send you a free gift that will help you understand and grow in your new relationship with the Lord. Welcome to your new life!

RECEIVE
THE HOLY SPIRIT

As His child, your loving heavenly Father wants to give you the supernatural power you need to live this new life.

> *For every one that asketh receiveth; and he that*
> *seeketh findeth; and to him that knocketh it shall*
> *be opened. . . . How much more shall your heavenly*
> *Father give the Holy Spirit to them that ask him?*
>
> **Luke 11:10 and 13b**

All you have to do is ask, believe, and receive!

Pray, "Father, I recognize my need for Your power to live this new life. Please fill me with Your Holy Spirit. By faith, I receive it right now! Thank You for baptizing me. Holy Spirit, You are welcome in my life!"

Congratulations! Now you're filled with God's supernatural power!

Some syllables from a language you don't recognize will rise up from your heart to your mouth (1 Cor. 14:14). As you speak them out loud by faith, you're releasing God's power from within and building yourself up in your spirit (1 Cor. 14:4). You can do this whenever and wherever you like.

It doesn't really matter whether you felt anything or not when you prayed to receive the Lord and His Spirit. If you believed in your heart that you received, then God's Word promises that you did. *"Therefore I say unto you, What things soever ye desire, when ye pray, believe that ye receive them, and ye shall have them"* (Mark 11:24). God always honors His Word—believe it!

Please contact our Helpline (719-635-1111) and let us know that you've prayed to be filled with the Holy Spirit. We would like to rejoice with you and help you understand more fully what has taken place in your life. We'll send you a free gift that will help you understand and grow in your new relationship with the Lord.

ABOUT THE AUTHOR

Andrew Wommack's life was forever changed the moment he encountered the supernatural love of God on March 23, 1968. As a renowned Bible teacher and author, Andrew has made it his mission to change the way the world sees God.

Andrew's vision is to go as far and deep with the Gospel as possible. His message goes far through the *Gospel Truth* television and radio program, which is available to nearly half the world's population. The message goes deep through discipleship at Charis Bible College, headquartered in Woodland Park, Colorado. Founded in 1994, Charis has campuses across the United States and around the globe.

Andrew also has an extensive library of teaching materials in print, audio, and video—most of which can be accessed for free from his website: **awmi.net**.

Contact Information

Andrew Wommack Ministries Inc.

PO Box 3333

Colorado Springs CO 80934-3333

Email: info@awmi.net

Helpline: 719-635-1111

Helpline Hours: 4:30 a.m. to 9:30 p.m. (MT)

awmi.net

FREE TEACHINGS

Andrew Wommack has a wealth of teaching materials just a click away! Watch a video, read a teaching article, or even download an audio teaching. From some of Andrew's early teachings to newer ones—covering a wide range of topics—**it's all available to you, completely free**!

Go to **awmi.net/popular** to start browsing today. Your life will never be the same!

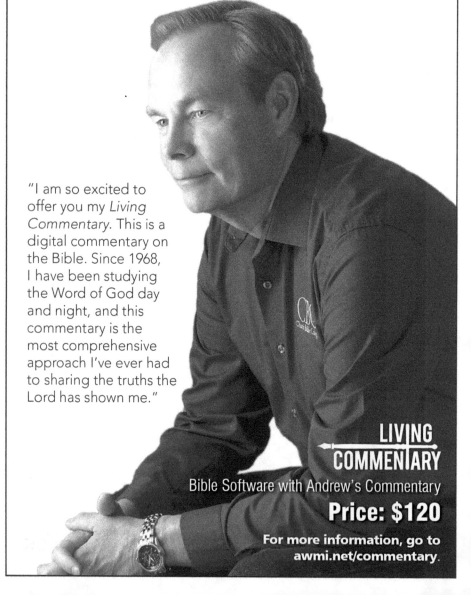

The Harrison House Vision

Proclaiming the truth and the power

of the Gospel of Jesus Christ with excellence.

Challenging Christians

to live victoriously,

grow spiritually,

know God intimately.

Connect with us on

Facebook @ HarrisonHousePublishers

and Instagram @ HarrisonHousePublishing

so you can stay up to date with news

about our books and our authors.

Visit us at **www.harrisonhouse.com**

for a complete product listing as well as

monthly specials for wholesale distribution.

Printed in the USA
CPSIA information can be obtained
at www.ICGtesting.com
LVHW061100120823
754344LV00014B/43